20,859

Days:

An Underdog Story

PHI   NE

41   **33**

By Brenden Peddigree

It was the day after Christmas in 1960. It was 20,859 days.

The professional football team from Philadelphia had been starved for a championship for decades, generations, what felt like forever. The Eagles had gone through 14 head coaches since Buck Shaw led the 1960 team to its championship. Thirty-seven different quarterbacks started games for the Eagles since Norm Van Brocklin hoisted the Championship trophy and retired to coaching after the 1960 season. 448 games ended with the Eagles on top, 446 ended with an L, 13 were ties. 21 seasons ended with a playoff loss. 18,207 regular season points were scored.

There were Eagles teams between 1960 and 2017 that had been close. The Eagles first Super Bowl trip came under Dick Vermeil in 1980. It was Vermeil's fifth season and the Eagles third straight season making the playoffs. The team beat the Vikings by 15 then the division-rival Cowboys by 13 to secure their Super Bowl berth. The 1980 squad boasted players like Ron Jaworski at quarterback, Wilbert Montgomery at running back and Harold Carmichael as the team's leading receiver. The defense also allowed the fewest points in the regular season and held their Super Bowl opponent Oakland Raiders to just seven points in their regular season match. The Eagles, however, fell short of the ultimate goal after an emotional victory against the Cowboys in the NFC Championship and only mustered 10 points. Raiders' quarterback Jim Plunkett had one of the best Super Bowl games to date while Jaworski had one of the worst. The Eagles lost 27-10 and didn't see another Super Bowl until the 2004 season.

There were a few years in the middle that they had a chance. In 1991 hearts around Philadelphia were broken during the opening weekend of the season. For an all-time defensive roster that had the likes of Reggie White, Jerome Brown, Clyde Simmons, Seth Joyner and Eric Allen all making the Pro Bowl, the offense didn't need to do much. However, they had a generational talent at quarterback in Randall Cunningham. In the Eagles' first game Cunningham tore his ACL, ending his season. "The Ultimate Weapon" was coming off of a season in which he was named Pro Football Writers of America's Most Valuable Player and a first-team All-Pro selection. The Eagles defense finished the season at the top of the NFL in passing yards allowed, rushing yards allowed and total yards allowed. They held opposing offenses to just 3.9 yards per play, 0.6 yards better than any other team that season. With Jim McMahon, Brad Goebel and Jeff Kemp as the team's quarterbacks, the Eagles fought their way to a 10-6 record that was good for third in the division. The season left fans wondering what could have been had Cunningham not gotten injured.

The early 2000s were a period of close-but-no-cigar for the Eagles. Starting in 2000 under second-year head coach Andy Reid and second-year quarterback Donovan McNabb, the Eagles went to the playoffs five straight years. From 2001-2003 the Eagles went to and lost three consecutive NFC Championships, each one in more heart-breaking fashion. Prior to the 2004 season, the Eagles completed a three-team trade that brought Terrell Owens to Philadelphia. Pairing Owens with McNabb and running back Brian Westbrook along with another Pro Bowl-infested defense, the Eagles had their best shot yet. The Eagles went 13-1 securing a first-round bye in the playoffs and homefield advantage before resting their starters for the final two games. However, after suffering a sprained ankle and fractured fibula against the Cowboys in week 15, the Eagles were without Owens for the final two games of the regular season and, likely, the playoffs as well. The Eagles finally got over the hump in 2004, defeating the Vikings and Falcons in the playoffs. They would meet the New England Patriots in the Super Bowl with the Patriots looking for their third Super Bowl victory in four seasons. Despite a surgery and pins in his leg,

Owens went against the better judgment of team doctors to play in the Super Bowl. His efforts were valiant with a nine-catch, 122-yard performance but the team fell short. McNabb threw three interceptions including one to Rodney Harrison on the final drive, sealing the Patriots 24-21. The Eagles loss made the Super Bowl LII victory that much sweeter as the Eagles finally got their revenge on head coach Bill Belichick and quarterback Tom Brady.

Over the years the Eagles brass has brought in or converted coaches to breathe new life into not only the organization but the league as a whole.

In 1976, the Eagles hired Dick Vermeil, a West Coast college coach for the previous 13 seasons, to take over for Mike McCormick who was the latest in a long line of bad coaches. Including McCormick's three seasons from 1973 to 1975, the Eagles hadn't had a winning record since 1966. Vermeil didn't exactly take the league by storm but starting in his third season he led the Eagles to four consecutive playoff berths including a trip to the Super Bowl in 1980. The Eagles fell short of the ultimate goal and two short years later Vermeil surprisingly retired.

Following three consecutive fourth-place-or-worse finishes in the NFC East, the Eagles hired the architect of one of the greatest defenses of all time to become their new head coach. Buddy Ryan, the inventor of the "46" defense and the coordinator of the daunting 1985 Chicago Bears defense, was hired after the Bears 46-10 domination of the New England Patriots in Super Bowl XX. After a 12-18-1 record in two seasons it appeared that Ryan may not have had what it took to make the leap from coordinator to head coach. In 1988, Ryan won the division and took the Eagles to the playoffs. The Eagles were one-and-done, losing to Ryan's former team, still head coached by Mike Ditka, 20-12. The Eagles did the same thing the next two years – losing in the first round of the playoffs in 1989 and 1990. Ryan's Eagles head coaching career came to a close after five years and a 0-3 playoff record in which his teams could only muster a total of 25 points in the three games. Ryan's lasting impression as Eagles head coach was his 8-2 record against the Dallas Cowboys.

In 2011, head coach Andy Reid left a lot of professionals scratching their heads when he hired Juan Castillo, an offensive line coach for 13 seasons with the Eagles, to be the defensive coordinator. Castillo hadn't coached on the defensive side of the ball in 22 years, and that was at the high school level. Reid, however, stood by his decision citing the fact that the late defensive coordinator Jim Johnson would often partner with Castillo in installing new schemes. The experiment lasted 22 games and Castillo was fired in October of 2012 after a 3-3 start. The Eagles would win just one more game that season and head coach Andy Reid, the coach for the last 14 seasons, was fired at the conclusion of the year.

Reid's replacement was another experiment. In 2013, Eagles owner Jeffrey Lurie hired Chip Kelly, then-head coach of the Oregon Ducks, to be the team's next head coach. Kelly was known for his hurry-up offensive style and had been a source for many NFL teams, including the Patriots, in bringing his up-tempo offense from college to the NFL. In the Eagles 2013 season opener against the Washington Redskins on Monday Night Football the world saw what the Eagles offense would look like. FAST is a word that shows up in big, bold letters as I look back in my notes from that game. It was a speed during plays, between plays, after plays that I had never seen before. Kelly took the league by surprise and became just the second head coach in NFL history to win his division in his first season. With a 10-6 record and a win over the Cowboys in the season finale, the Eagles were back in the playoffs after a two-year hiatus. The league caught on to Kelly in 2014 and he still managed to repeat with a 10-6 record but did not make the playoffs. When Kelly gained full control over the Eagles player personnel decisions, disaster ensued. Kelly traded away LeSean McCoy, the Eagles all-time leading rusher, for a linebacker. He traded Nick Foles, the quarterback responsible for a seven-touchdown performance and the eventual Super Bowl MVP, for Sam Bradford, a player who is now on his third team in four years. Chip Kelly the GM sent Howie Roseman to a separate wing of the building and sent iconic franchise players packing. His final season as Eagles head coach and GM saw him going 6-9 and being fired before the team's final game. Another failed experiment.

The aforementioned stars that Kelly sent packing were just some of the superstars who passed through Philadelphia, sold some jerseys, made their mark on the city but failed to bring home a Lombardi Trophy.

Quarterbacks

Randall Cunningham, the "Ultimate Weapon," was with the Eagles for 11 seasons and was named to three Pro Bowls as an Eagle. He was named to the All-Pro team three times, once as a first-teamer. Cunningham is responsible for countless highlights from keeping plays alive with his feet to 95-yard touchdown passes to 91-yard punts (yeah, he had a leg too). However, when it came to the postseason, Cunningham's 1-5 record left Eagles fans wanting more from the quarterback who had a .607 win percentage as a starting quarterback.

When Donovan McNabb came to the Eagles in 1999 there were shades of Cunningham with his ability to extend plays with his feet. McNabb's streak from 2000-2004 are arguably the best five years any Eagles quarterback, or any Eagles team, has had to date. With five consecutive Pro Bowl selections and seven postseason wins, McNabb quickly solidified himself as the best quarterback in franchise history. Despite the years of success, McNabb will always be remembered as someone who consistently came close but couldn't get over the hump. There will always be the question of whether or not McNabb threw up during the biggest game of his career before throwing a game-ending interception to lose Super Bowl XXXIX.

Michael Vick was signed by the Eagles after his release from prison that was a result in his involvement in a dog fighting ring. After a year as the Eagles third-string quarterback and the team's trade of McNabb before the 2010 season, Vick was one play away from the being the Eagles starting quarterback. That play came in the 2010 season opener and Vick took the opportunity and, quite literally, ran with it. Vick was named a Pro Bowler and the NFL's Comeback Player of the Year and had one of the best games by an Eagles quarterback. On Monday Night Football, Vick took over in a 59-28 rout of the Washington Redskins. Vick threw for 333 yards and added another 80 on the ground while accounting for six total touchdowns – four passing and two rushing. Vick is responsible for some of the most exciting quarterback play in Eagles history but he wasn't the quarterback to take the Eagles over the hump.

Running backs

Brian Westbrook played his collegiate career at Villanova and was drafted by the Eagles in the third round in 2002. Westbrook quickly became a triple threat for the Eagles, excelling as a runner, receiver and special teams player. His best season came in 2007 when he was a Pro Bowler and was name first-team All-Pro. With over 1,300 yards on the ground and nearly 800 receiving yards, Westbrook accounted for 12 touchdowns. Westbrook set the Eagles franchise record for receptions in a season in 2007 with 90 catches that still stands today. The drafting of a second-round running back in 2009 spelled the end for Westbrook who had his lowest rushing and receiving totals since his rookie season. After a one-year stint in San Francisco, Westbrook retired as a member of the Eagles and was named to the Eagles Hall of Fame in 2015.

The running back who replaced Westbrook was none other than LeSean McCoy. A specialist in making defenders miss, McCoy became a 1,000-yard rusher in his first year as a full-time starter in 2010. A year later, in 2011, McCoy couldn't keep out of the endzone and broke the Eagles franchise record with 20 total touchdowns. The record stood for 66 years before McCoy broke it and was named first-team All-Pro in the process. McCoy earned his second All-Pro selection in 2013 when he averaged over 100 rushing yards per game and led the league with 2,146 total yards. McCoy's Eagles career ended a season later when Chip Kelly traded the superstar running back for a linebacker with potential. McCoy finished his Eagles career as the franchise leader in rushing yards in just six seasons with 6,792 total rushing yards. The running back was never a part of a postseason victory as an Eagle.

Wide receivers

Harold Carmichael was a seventh-round pick by the Eagles in 1971. Carmichael, towering his peers at 6-8, looked like he belonged on a basketball court rather than on the gridiron. His height gave him a distinct advantage that he used on his way to four Pro Bowls, three second-team All-Pro selections and a spot on the 1970s All-Decade team. Carmichael was second on the Eagles in receptions and led the team in receiving touchdowns in 1980. Number 17 finished his career with 589 receptions, 8,985 receiving yards and 79 touchdowns, all of which still stand as Eagles records.

When the Eagles made a three-team trade that netted a wide receiver that had 5,265 receiving yards and 51 touchdowns over the previous four seasons, they were making a statement. The statement was that they were finished being runner-ups in the NFC after three consecutive NFC Championship Game losses. They stood by their statement and got over the hump despite Terrell Owens, their prized offseason acquisition, not playing throughout the playoffs. Owens still holds the Eagles single-season record for touchdown catches in a season with 14. His Eagles career was short-lived, though as he sought to re-negotiate his contract in 2005 and had a falling out with multiple Eagles including McNabb and Hugh Douglas. Owens has since been inducted into the Hall of Fame and could have had a long, illustrious career in Philadelphia had he kept some things to himself. That's not TO, though, and his 22-game Eagles career left fans wondering what could have been...once again.

Defenders

The Eagles made a blockbuster trade in 1974, sending two first-round picks and a second-round pick to the Cincinnati Bengals to acquire linebacker Bill Bergey. Bergey's performance over the next seven years made many forget what the Eagles gave up to acquire the superstar. After not being named to an All-Pro team in his five seasons as a Bengal, Bergey started his Eagles career by being named to the All-Pro team five consecutive seasons, twice on the first-team. As the Eagles defense rose to being one of the best in the league, Bergey was at the center of it all. Number 66 retired following the Eagles Super Bowl XV loss in 1980 having been named to five Pro Bowls and entered both the Eagles and Philadelphia Sports Halls of Fame.

After a 5-10-1 season in head coach Buddy Ryan's inaugural season as head coach, the Eagles had a top ten pick in the 1987 draft. The Eagles used that selection to draft Jerome Brown, a defensive tackle out of Miami. From the moment he stepped onto the field, it was clear that the Eagles drafted a future star. Brown tallied up 19.5 sacks in his first three seasons as an Eagle and the team's defense once again was on the rise. In 1990 and 1991 Brown recovered seven fumbles and notched 10 sacks as the Eagles became the top defense in the league. Brown was named to the Pro Bowl and the All-Pro team in both seasons. Prior to the 1992 season tragedy struck and Brown passed away in a car accident in his hometown of Brooksville, Florida. At 27 years old the Eagles lost not only a terrific football player but one of the central members of the team and always brought laughter to his teammates and those around him. So much so that players didn't believe the news of his death and thought it was another elaborate joke that Brown was playing on his teammates. The Eagles lost a family member when Brown passed but not before he left his legacy on the community, his teammates and one of the best defenses in league history.

Reggie White is the greatest Eagles player in the history of the franchise. Plain and simple, no matter how you look at it, Reggie is number one. From the moment he stepped on the field as a rookie in 1985, White was a man playing among boys. White recorded double-digit sacks in his first nine seasons in the league including an average of 17.5 sacks in his first four seasons in the NFL. White was the engine of the Eagles defense in his eight seasons in Philadelphia, going to seven Pro Bowls and earning six first-team All-Pro selections. Following the 1992 season, White hit free agency and in one of the most controversial moves in team history, the Eagles allowed White to walk, where he signed with the Green Bay Packers. White won a Super Bowl in Green Bay in 1996 but was never quite the player as a Packer as he was with the Eagles. As an Eagle, number 92 averaged 15.5 sacks per season. As a Packer, he averaged 11.4 in six seasons. Despite not winning a ring as an Eagle, White still solidified himself as the greatest Eagle of all-time and will forever be remembered as the Minister of the greatest defense in Eagles history.

If there were one Eagle who deserved to win a ring more than any other in the franchise's history it would be Brian Dawkins. Weapon X finally did win a ring as a member of the Eagles front office but it would have been a site to see had he won it on the field. Dawkins exemplified the city of Philadelphia since he arrived in 1996 to his departure, another controversial one, in 2008. Dawkins was the heart and soul of the elite Eagles defenses of the early 2000s and allowed legendary defensive coordinator Jim Johnson to design never-before-seen defensive schemes. Dawkins wasn't the biggest, strongest or fastest player in the league but he put his body on the line every down and every second he was on the field. He always said that he played every game as if an Eagles fan got the opportunity to play one game and put everything he had into that game. The attitude endeared him to the city he played in. Dawkins finished his career with 37 interceptions, 36 forced fumbles, 26 sacks, nine Pro Bowls and five first-team All-Pro selections. On the day before Super Bowl LII it was announced that Dawkins was selected as a member of the Pro Football Hall of Fame's class of 2018. The next day, Dawkins was finally able to hoist the Lombardi Trophy as the most deserving Eagle in franchise history.

****

All of these Eagles will be remembered in the team's history as legends. None of them, however, were able to bring the Lombardi to the city of Philadelphia. The 2017 Eagles had a number of stars who will eventually be legends as well.

The players who made up the 2017 roster formed a brotherhood through blood, sweat and tears. Through injury and criticism they had each other. "We all we got, we all we need," became a mantra true to the squad. The road to the Eagles first Super Bowl in franchise history couldn't have been scripted any better.

Franchise quarterback tears his ACL. Hall of Fame left tackle tears his ACL. Heart of the defense tears his Achilles. Homerun-hitting running back tears his ACL and breaks his arm on the same play. Special teams ace tears his ACL. "Least qualified head coach" in decades leading the squad. Facing the greatest head coach and quarterback of all-time in the Super Bowl. Underdogs throughout the playoffs.

Underdogs. That is the one that stuck. The Eagles clung onto the title and used it to motivate them from December 10th, the day MVP-hopeful Carson Wentz was lost for the season, to February 4th, the day their backup quarterback elevated the Lombardi Trophy as the Super Bowl MVP.

The Eagles underdog moniker was accompanied with masks, headlines and eventually an engraving on the Super Bowl jewelry. The theme didn't just match the team, it matched the individuals from the top of the organization to the bottom.

Howie Roseman
Executive Vice President of Football Operations

Roseman has been to hell and back with the Philadelphia Eagles. Following the Super Bowl victory, he was residing on top of the world.

Roseman's Eagles story dates back to high school when he began sending letters to all 32 NFL teams. When he was nine or ten years old, he wasn't the kid who wanted to be a firefighter or police officer. Whenever he was asked, Roseman told people he wanted to be the general manager of an NFL team. He knew it wouldn't come easy. His letters continued through college at the University of Florida and Fordham University law school. The letters, which were being sent almost weekly, were fruitless until 1999, when Roseman was 24, when the New York Jets offered him an internship. One year later, Roseman had his foot in the door with the Eagles.

From 2000 to 2002, Roseman served as an intern with the title of salary cap counselor. Slowly but surely, Roseman worked and worked and climbed the ladder all within the Eagles organization, a rarity in the NFL when promotions often come with different teams. Roseman's childhood dream finally came to fruition in 2010 when a mentor of his, general manager Tom Heckert left Philadelphia for the same role with the Cleveland Browns. Roseman took over and became the youngest general manager in league history at just 34 years old.

Roseman served his first three years as an advisor to Head Coach Andy Reid, who had the final say in all football decisions. When the Eagles and Reid parted ways, Roseman was instrumental in bringing Oregon head coach Chip Kelly to Philadelphia.

For two seasons, Kelly and Roseman worked hand-in-hand. Kelly, like Reid, had final say on roster decisions but there appeared to be no disconnect between general manager and head coach. Despite releasing players like Evan Mathis and DeSean Jackson and trading LeSean McCoy and Nick Foles, all fan-favorites and Pro Bowlers, Roseman and Kelly were working together.

In 2015, the power struggle came to a breaking point and Roseman was stripped of his general manager title and was "elevated" to Executive Vice President of Football operations. The title came with a move of his office that took him away from the player personnel side of the building.

After being banished to the opposite side of the Eagles facility, Eagles center Jason Kelce stated two years late in an impassioned speech on the steps of the Philadelphia Art Museum that the players rarely saw Roseman. In exile and no longer heading football decisions, Roseman took a year to learn from executives in the MLB, NBA, NHL, English Premier League and even outside of sports. What he gained helped him craft the roster that took the Eagles to the Super Bowl. It took tough decisions – ones that kept him up at night – but he always deferred to an adage from former Green Bay Packers GM Ron Wolf.

Ron Wolf stated that if you are hitting on 60 percent of your decisions, you're going to be an unbelievable executive in the NFL. Roseman said that he learned to accept failure and research the bad decisions and make sure they don't happen again. As long as the good decisions outweigh the bad ones, he was doing well.

Roseman's learning tour served him well and in 2016, he was back in the fold making personnel decisions with a new outlook on the decision-making process.

When Kelly was fired and Pederson took the helm, Roseman once again came to the forefront. He has worked wonders in years past with aggressive trades and salary cap maneuvering but no offseason was more impressive than 2017's.

Roseman's list of acquisitions looks like the Eagles MVP list for the 2017 season. In addition to signing Nick Foles, Alshon Jeffery and LeGarrette Blount, all of who scored touchdowns in the Super Bowl, Roseman also had his hands in drafting Derek Barnett (recovered Tom Brady's fourth-quarter fumble in the Super Bowl), trading for Jay Ajayi (254 total yards in playoffs) and signing Corey Clement (100 receiving yards, TD in the Super Bowl) as an undrafted rookie free agent. Players acquired by Roseman prior to the 2017 season were responsible for 88 of the Eagles' 94 points in the postseason.

Without Roseman in his current role, and going to hell and back within the organization, the Eagles perhaps don't even make it to the Super Bowl let alone win it. As one of few members of the organization who was around during the 2004 Super Bowl, Roseman made certain that the outcome of this trip would be different.

Doug Pederson
Head Coach

Doug Pederson has been in the background nearly his whole football career. Attending Northeast Louisiana University, now University of Louisiana – Monroe, Pederson's quarterbacking records for the school didn't mean much with the limited exposure he got. Even the way Pederson got the quarterback position at ULM was by chance. Pederson's father Gordon was being transferred from Washington state to Louisiana for work. Gordon Pederson mentioned to ULM Head Coach Pat Collins that his son was a quarterback and was planning on taking some film to Louisiana Tech in hopes of getting a position on the team. After watching the film and hearing that they were looking at Louisiana Tech, Collins immediately offered Doug Pederson a scholarship.

Pederson's highlights include over 6,000 career passing yards, 619 of which came in one game, and a Division I-AA Championship in which Pederson dressed only for special teams. These weren't enough to earn him a draft slot and he signed with the Miami Dolphins as an undrafted rookie free agent. His first five seasons in the NFL (1991-95) included being released by the Dolphins seven times, a three-month period as a Carolina Panther after the expansion draft and two stints in the World League of American Football.

Pederson finally found some stability when he was signed by the Green Bay Packers in November of 1995. This is where the quarterback first met Andy Reid, who coached the Packers' offensive line. Pederson battled for the next two seasons, making the roster as the third-string quarterback. In 1998, Pederson finally moved up the depth chart to primary backup and saw the field as the team's placekick holder. Through 1998, Pederson had a grand total of 32 pass attempts in the NFL. In 1999, Pederson got his shot at a starting role.

When the Eagles signed little-known quarterback coach Andy Reid to be their head coach, Reid brought Pederson along with him to be the team's starting quarterback. Reid had coached Pederson in 1997 and 1998 after being promoted to quarterbacks coach in Green Bay. When Reid drafted quarterback Donovan McNabb with the second overall pick, he reiterated that Pederson would start until McNabb was ready. Pederson started and completed five of the Eagles first nine games of the 1999 season, giving way to McNabb to see action in four of those games due to injury or poor play. With a 23-0 deficit at halftime of the Eagles week nine game against the Panthers, Pederson was benched for good. McNabb became the Eagles starter for the next ten years. Pederson spent the 2000 training camp with the Eagles but was released before the regular season, leading him to contemplate retirement.

Pederson got another shot in 2000 with the Cleveland Browns as the third-string quarterback. After a rash of injuries, Pederson ended up starting eight games for Cleveland in place of Tim Couch and Spergon Wynn. The year 2000 concluded Pederson's NFL starts, checking in with a career record of 3-14 as a starter.

From 2001 through 2004, Pederson resigned with the Packers, serving as the primary backup to Brett Favre as well as holding placekicks. In a 2004 game, Pederson took a shot to his side that cracked a bone in his back, tore a muscle in his torso and broke a rib. Pederson finished the game but the injury landed him on injured reserve. The career-backup retired following the 2004 season to coach high school football.

Fast forward to 2009 and Pederson made his way back to the NFL as an offensive quality control coach for his former quarterbacks coach and head coach, Andy Reid. It took just two years until Pederson was coaching the quarterbacks. Two years later, he got another promotion to offensive coordinator. This came in Kansas City when the Eagles and Andy Reid parted ways and Reid became the head coach of the Chiefs.

Pederson got his shot at NFL head coach in 2016 when the Eagles hired him to replace Chip Kelly. Pederson was reportedly one of the last options for the Eagles. According to some media outlets, the Eagles wanted either Adam Gase or Ben McAdoo but settled for the former Chiefs offensive coordinator. Gase is on the hot seat in Miami with a .500 record in his first two seasons while McAdoo is unemployed.

After drafting quarterback Carson Wentz with the second overall pick, the Eagles set their depth chart with Sam Bradford and Chase Daniel ahead of the rookie. On September 3rd, Minnesota Vikings quarterback Teddy Bridgewater suffered a season-ending knee injury and came to the Eagles calling for a quarterback. The Eagles obliged, sending Bradford to the Vikings and naming Wentz, not Daniel, the starting quarterback.

Pederson and Wentz set the league on fire in the first three weeks of the season, starting 3-0 with a dominating victory over the AFC-powerhouse Pittsburgh Steelers in week three. The season took a turn for the worst after that, having the Eagles lose nine of their next eleven games and finishing the season 7-9 at the bottom of the NFC East.

The offseason was filled with speculation as to whether or not Pederson was the long-term answer at head coach. Was his coaching detrimental to the development of their young, franchise quarterback? Was he just a place-holder until the Eagles found their guy? Was that guy Pederson's defensive coordinator Jim Schwartz whose defense allowed fewer than 21 points per game?

Pederson's 2017 season began and ended with a victory and a Gatorade bath. After a season-opening victory the Eagles bathed their coach in Gatorade for a job-well-done. Pederson spent much of his offseason being questioned and ridiculed by football "experts." A certain former-GM called Pederson the least-qualified coach in the last 30 years. All the while, Pederson's team stuck by his side and rewarded their head coach for his first of what would become 16 victories that season.

A few weeks into the season NFL Films caught an exchange between Pederson and Brandon Graham toward the end of the game in which Pederson jokingly told Graham that the team is "overcoming the coaching," a clear jab at the experts still questioning Pederson's merits.

In week three, Darren Sproles suffered two injuries on the same play that shut him down for the year. In week six, special teams ace Chris Maragos was lost for the season. In week seven, Jason Peters and Jordan Hicks both went down for the season. In week fourteen, the Eagles lost their MVP, Carson Wentz, for the year.

As long as the Eagles had the unlikely head coach, they would overcome. Pederson won the Eagles locker room early with his postgame speeches that would make Knute Rockne proud. Late in the season, he was the leader that the Eagles needed to set aside the adversity. His "We Ain't Done...YET" chants became a war cry for the Eagles down the stretch.

For Pederson to overcome all of the team's injuries to win the first Super Bowl was simply incredible. His game-planning made Nick Foles look like an All-Pro quarterback and eventually led to him winning a shootout with the greatest quarterback of all time in the team's biggest game of all time. The least-qualified coach of the last 30 years outdueled the likes of Bill Belichick, Matt Patricia and Josh McDaniels.

Pederson's football story went from journeyman NFL backup quarterback to high school head coach to NFL quarterback coach, NFL offensive coordinator and finally getting his first head coaching gig with Philadelphia, a city he played and assistant-coached in. A mere eight years removed from high school coaching, Pederson stood victorious on the sport's grandest stage, hoisting the Lombardi Trophy.

Nick Foles
Quarterback

9

Wow. I mean what can you say? Foles almost quit football in 2015 after a wretched season in St. Louis that included two benchings and more turnovers than touchdowns.

The quarterback was on top of the world following his 27-touchdown, 2-interception and Pro Bowl MVP 2013 season in just his second year in the league. Some attribute the season to the offense that then-head coach Chip Kelly installed but Foles has taken care of the football dating back to college, boasting at least a 2:1 touchdown:interception ratio in each of his three seasons at Arizona. Additionally, Foles has stuck around in the NFL and, at the time of this writing, Chip Kelly is the head coach of UCLA.

Following his historical season, Foles entered 2014 as the Eagles starting quarterback. After a season of just four turnovers in 2013, Foles nearly matched that total in the first half of the Eagles season-opener of 2014 with two lost fumbles and an interception. The Eagles ended up winning the game but it previewed a struggle that Foles would have throughout the season. Foles appeared in just eight games in 2014, being lost midway through the season with a broken collarbone. He compiled a 6-2 record despite having as many turnovers as touchdowns. Following the 2014 season, Foles was dealt to the St. Louis Rams in a deal that brought Sam Bradford to Philadelphia.

The Rams were head-coached by Jeff Fisher at the time and the roster had quarterbacks Sean Mannion and Case Keenum along with Foles. Keenum and Foles, who grew close during their time with the team, would later meet in the 2017 NFC Championship Game.

After receiving a two-year extension from the Rams following the trade, Foles entered 2015 as the unquestioned starter. Foles began his season on a high note, leading the Rams to an overtime, divisional victory over the Seattle Seahawks in the season opener. Prior to the victory, the Rams had been 2-7 in their last nine games against the Seahawks.

The rest of the 2015 season didn't go as well as the Rams' opener. Foles struggled to find a rhythm with his new team, losing the next two games before bouncing back against the Arizona Cardinals, bringing the Rams to a 2-2 record. Foles' next five games were some of the worst of his career. The Rams went 2-3 and Foles threw just two touchdowns to five interceptions in that stretch. With the Rams sitting at 4-5, Fisher decided to bench Foles in favor of Keenum.

A concussion in Keenum's first game as starter forced Foles back into the starting role. Foles went 0-2 in two games while Keenum recovered, throwing four interceptions and failing to throw a touchdown pass. Keenum returned in week 13 and Foles' spent the rest of the season on the bench. In Foles' final seven games as a starter he threw just two touchdowns with nine interceptions leading the Rams to a 2-5 record. Benched and defeated, Foles began to question his NFL future.

The Rams, now in Los Angeles, selected Jared Goff with the first overall pick in the 2016 draft which led to Foles requesting his release from the team. His release was granted and Foles was a free agent for the first time in his career. After his rough 2015 season, Foles' market wasn't exactly abuzz.

After the worst season of Foles' career, he decided that he would only return to football for one coach: Andy Reid, the coach who drafted him back in 2012. Reid obliged and brought Foles in as a backup for the Kansas City Chiefs in 2016. When Foles hit free-agency following the 2016 season, he decided to join Reid's disciple in the town that originally drafted him.

Foles served as a clipboard-holder for the first 12 games of the 2017 season in Philadelphia. He had thrown just four passes on the season after missing the entire preseason and a large portion of training camp. Foles came in to relieve injured-Carson Wentz against Los Angeles and closed out the game with a victory that helped secure the NFC East and homefield advantage in the playoffs. He followed that up with a four-touchdown performance against the New York Giants followed by a few discouraging outings against the Oakland Raiders and Dallas Cowboys.

Due to Foles' less-than-stellar track record, the Eagles headed into the divisional round, conference championship and even the Super Bowl as underdogs. Foles got better each game after the coaching staff studied what made him so successful in 2013.

He finished each of those games with 100.1, 141.4 and 106.1 passer ratings. He threw six touchdowns and his only interception came on a tipped ball. He executed the run-pass-option to near-perfection, slicing defenses in his wake.

Foles was also on the receiving end of arguably the greatest play in Super Bowl history and undoubtedly one of the two most memorable plays in Eagles history. After rushing to the sideline on a 4th-and-goal timeout, Foles suggested to Doug Pederson the Eagles run "Philly, Philly" (later clarified that the play was actually called the "Philly Special"). Pederson agreed and Foles and the Eagles executed the play to perfection. The direct snap went to rookie running back Corey Clement who took the ball left. A reversing-Trey Burton then received the pitch from Clement. According to Burton, coaches advised him that his first three options on the play were run, run and run. With Foles wide open, Burton lobbed the ball up and Foles came down with the first touchdown reception by a quarterback in Super Bowl history.

Foles followed that up by delivering pinpoint-accurate touchdowns to Alshon Jeffery and Clement. The backup completed the game with 373 yards, three touchdowns and an interception on a tipped pass while completing 65 percent of his 43 pass attempts. Of course, he also added the one-yard touchdown reception as well. The game was placed in Foles' hands and he answered the call with the game of his life.

Many called the Eagles dead when Wentz went down and were certain they would go one-and-done. The Falcons had too great of a defensive rush, they said. The Vikings were the best defense in the league, Foles hasn't seen anything like this, they said. This team didn't stand a chance against the GOAT quarterback and coach and the evil empire, they said. Foles silenced the nay-sayers and performed at an elite level throughout the playoffs.

The goofy quarterback who nearly quit football two seasons earlier went toe-to-toe with the greatest quarterback of all-time and came out on top, celebrating the victory and the Super Bowl MVP title with his wife and infant daughter.

LeGarrette Blount
Running Back

29

Blount has been overlooked as far back as high school when he recorded three straight 1,000-yard rushing seasons but was only a two-star recruit and failed to get a scholarship offer. He attended football camp at Auburn University but was not offered a scholarship. At that point, Blount chose to attend Auburn anyway and his football career almost came to an end right there.

However, Blount was not academically qualified to attend Auburn and was forced to attend East Mississippi Community College where he joined the football team. He surpassed 1,000 yards in each of his two seasons, scored 18 touchdowns and was named to the Junior College All-American team. Finally, the recruiting was there for Blount. Blount committed to Oregon in 2007.

In Blount's junior season he averaged at least five yards per carry in 11 of 13 games – including more than 10 yards per carry in three games – while splitting time at running back. Blount finished the season with 1,000 yards and set the single-season school record with 17 rushing touchdowns. Then, Blount ran into some issues.

Following the 2008 season, Blount was suspended for skipping multiple workouts. The suspension sent a message to Blount and he was reinstated by new Oregon head coach Chip Kelly, heading into the 2009 season as the lead back.

The Ducks opened the season against Boise State and Blount rushed for -5 yards on eight carries. The running back was clearly frustrated with his performance and when a Boise State player approached him following the game, Blount threw a punch that knocked that player to the ground and caused more trouble for himself. He was initially suspended for the remainder of the season, ending his college football career. The suspension was withdrawn in November and Blount was active for the final four games of the season, including the Rose Bowl. Blount registered just 82 yards on the season, severely diminishing his draft stock.

Blount went undrafted in the 2010 NFL Draft and signed with the Tennessee Titans as an undrafted rookie free agent. The former Duck survived final roster cuts but was released to make room for two players the Titans signed from other teams' cuts. Blount was claimed off waivers by the Tampa Bay Buccaneers, where he would spend the first three seasons of his NFL career.

Blount's rookie season was a redemption tour for being undrafted and released by the Titans. He rushed for over 1,000 yards and led all rookie running backs in rushing in 2010 and became just the second undrafted rookie to rush for over 1,000 yards in his first season.

Blount followed up his rookie season with a strong sophomore season as the Buccaneers lead back. Blount finished the season with nearly 800 rushing yards and an increased role in the passing game. His third season with the Bucs saw him receive a greatly diminished role as Doug Martin stormed into the league.

Following the 2012 season Blount was traded to the New England Patriots for a seventh-round pick and running back Jeff Demps, who concluded his NFL career with one carry.

Blount spent 2013 as a part of the Patriot's running back rotation that included himself, Stevan Ridley, Brandon Bolden and Shane Vereen. Blount finished the season one yard behind Ridley with 772 yards on the season and tied Ridley for the team lead with seven touchdowns. When Blount's contract expired, the Patriots decided to let him walk. He signed a two-year contract with the Steelers, where Blount found more trouble.

Before the 2014 season, Blount was caught, with Steelers running back LeVeon Bell, with 20 grams of marijuana in the car they were driving in. Both players were arrested for marijuana possession and Blount's stint with the Steelers was off to a poor start.

Blount's Steelers career lasted just eleven games. He failed to rush for 30 yards in all but one of them. Blount's worst game came against the New York Jets when he failed to gain any yards on five carries. One week later, he didn't register a carry and out of frustration, headed to the locker room prior to the game hitting 0:00. The next day, Blount was released.

Blount's free agency didn't last long. Four days after his release, his old team came calling. For the final five games of the season, Blount was a Patriot.

After averaging just 24 yards per game with the Steelers, Blount averaged 56 yards per game over his final five games. Blount's release from the Steelers was a blessing in disguise. In the AFC Championship Game, the Patriots rode Blount to the tune of 30 carries for 148 yards and three touchdowns. Two weeks later, Blount and the Patriots hoisted the Lombardi.

Blount spent the next two seasons with New England, missing out on the 2015 playoffs due to a hip injury. In his 30-year-old season in 2016, Blount led the league with 18 rushing touchdowns and had his first 1,000-yard rushing season since his rookie year of 2010. He was the primary back in the Patriots run to a 14-2 season and the franchise's fifth Super Bowl (Blount's second).

After a stellar season with the New England Patriots in 2016, Blount was asked to take a pay cut if he planned on returning to the team that had supplied him with two Super Bowl titles in three years.

Blount decided to bet on himself in the offseason, refusing a pay cut from the Patriots and testing the market to find a new employer. Two months into free agency, Blount found his suitor in Philadelphia.

Upon signing, Blount was immediately penciled in as the starter. The 31-year-old back rewarded the Eagles confidence in him by leading the team in rushing and delivering earthquake-like highlights like his 68-yard "beast mode" run against the Los Angeles Chargers. Blount failed to come close to his 2016 touchdown production with only three touchdowns. However, he scored when it counted.

Blount scored touchdowns in each of the Eagles' postseason games including a 21-yard touchdown in the Super Bowl against his former team. From the moment Blount burst through the hole to the spike of the ball after the score, you could see Blount's motivation to get into the endzone against the team who thought he wasn't worth his paycheck. Blount's 90 rushing yards were good for the most in the game.

Blount matched his regular season total of three touchdowns in three playoff games. The running back, even at the NFL-equivalent of "ancient" was well worth the money the Eagles invested and ultimately earned his paycheck with a single touchdown that helped give the Eagles their first Super Bowl in franchise history.

Not bad for a guy who was almost forced quit football at 18 years old.

Jay Ajayi
Running Back

36

After spending the first seven years of his life in London, Jay Ajayi and his family moved to the football capital of the world. In Texas, Ajayi picked up American sports shortly after coming to the states and was a letterman in both football and track and field. As a senior, Ajayi earned second-team all-state honors after averaging 10 yards per carry on his way to a 2,240-yard, 35-touchdown season.

Ajayi took his talents to Boise State where he was redshirted his freshman season. Ajayi ran into some trouble in October of his freshman year when he attempted to steal clothes from Walmart. He was sentenced to five days in jail for the crime.

When Ajayi finally saw the field in 2012, he was the backup to running back DJ Harper. On just 82 carries, Ajayi finished with the highest yards per carry average (6.7) by a running back in the Mountain West Conference.

In his sophomore and junior seasons, Ajayi was the lone back to lead the Broncos. As a two-year starter, Ajayi compiled 3,248 yards and 48 touchdowns on the ground, adding 757 receiving yards and another five touchdowns. As a junior, Ajayi became the only player in FBS history to rush for more than 1,800 yards while having more than 500 receiving yards. Following his dominant two years, Ajayi decided to forego his senior season and enter the 2015 NFL Draft.

Despite Ajayi's dominance, he was still the 14th running back taken in the draft. There were 12 running backs and a full back selected ahead of Ajayi's fifth-round draft slot in 2015. However, the running back has outplayed almost all of those backs in his first three seasons in the NFL. Only two running backs drafted ahead of his have more rushing yards than Ajayi while only four have more touchdowns. The two backs who have more rushing yards than Ajayi – Todd Gurley and Melvin Gordon – were the only two running backs selected in the first round that season. Ajayi undoubtedly used his draft position as motivation.

In his rookie season, Ajayi missed seven games due to an injury sustained in the Dolphins' final preseason game. Upon returning, Ajayi only notched 49 carries and 187 yards.

Had it not been for an injury and subsequent mid-season retirement by Dolphins starting running back Arian Foster during the 2016 season, Ajayi's career could have turned out very differently. Following the 2015 season, Dolphins lead running back Lamar Miller departed in free agency for the Houston Texans. Ajayi was next up on the depth chart but before even getting the chance to be the starter was relegated once again when Foster took over as starter during training camp.

Ajayi was frustrated with once again being the backup and didn't hide it. First-year head coach Adam Gase made the decision to deactivate Ajayi and leave him in Miami for the season opener against the Seattle Seahawks. In the first three games following his return, Ajayi only had 18 carries for 75 yards. With Foster suffering a hamstring injury Ajayi's role increased, only slightly at first. Ajayi saw 13 carries in his fourth game of the season. Then Ajayi showed his coach that the wrong decision was made not naming him starter.

Ajayi helped spark a six-game win streak and 9-2 record to close out the season after a 1-4 start. In Ajayi's first two games as the feature back he ran for 204 and 214 yards. He became just the fourth player in NFL history to rush for 200 or more yards in back-to-back games. Ajayi followed that up with another 100-yard performance, accumulating 529 yards and four touchdowns in a three-game stretch. Following Ajayi's second 200-yard performance, Foster announced his retirement from the NFL and the job was Ajayi's with nobody breathing down his neck.

Ajayi added a third 200-yard performance in week 16 becoming one of 15 players to have at least three 200-yard rushing performances in their career. Ajayi did it in ¾ of a season as a full-time starter. The running back's dominant 2016 season earned him a trip to the Pro Bowl.

To begin the 2017 season, Ajayi was the Dolphins lead back but reports of issues with team chemistry and buy-in arose out of Miami. Ajayi reportedly was unhappy with the number of carries he was receiving, even after Dolphins' wins, and expressed his displeasure to his position coach. He was also referenced, albeit not by name, when head coach Adam Gase said "guys have got to actually take this stuff home and study it." When the trade deadline came, the Dolphins made their move and none other than Howie Roseman was on the other end of it. The Eagles completed a blockbuster trade at the deadline on October 31st when they sent a fourth-round pick to Miami in exchange for the Pro Bowl running back.

Ajayi, exiled from the team that drafted him and reports abound regarding the reasons for his departure, burst into the Eagles backfield in his first game as an Eagle. On just eight carries, Ajayi ran for 77 yards including a 46-yard touchdown. The newest Eagle followed that up with a 91-yard performance against the Dallas Cowboys including a 71-yard run. In his first two games as an Eagle, Ajayi averaged 11.2 yards per carry. Some punishment that turned out to be.

Ajayi came up big when the Eagles needed him most. He led the way in the backfield, carrying the load for the final three games of the season. When the playoffs came, Ajayi continued his lead. Against the Atlanta Falcons in the divisional round, he ran for 54 yards, adding another 44 yards on three receptions. He added another 99 total yards against the Minnesota Vikings in the NFC Championship Game. Finally, Ajayi ran for 57 yards in the Super Bowl, second only to his backfield mate LeGarrette Blount.

Getting Ajayi for a fourth-round pick was a steal for the Eagles. Being discarded from the team that drafted him only to win a Super Bowl with his new team was a steal for Ajayi.

Corey Clement
Running Back

30

It could be argued that Clement is the biggest underdog on the Eagles 2017 Super Bowl squad. His journey has been something you couldn't script any better.

Growing up in Glassboro, NJ, Clement rooted for the Eagles until Terrell Owens departed for the Cowboys. Then, Clement's allegiance followed Owens to Dallas. The running back did, however, post a photo on Twitter of a visit to the NovaCare Complex where Clement's caption read "One day...Some day." The photo, from 2012 when Clement was just 17 years old, turned out to be prophetic.

After accumulating over 6,000 yards and 90 total touchdowns at Glassboro High School, Clement was rated as a four-star recruit and a top-20 running back in the nation. After initially committing to Pittsburgh, Clement later withdrew his commitment and chose to attend Wisconsin instead despite a stronger running back group with the Badgers.

Clement's freshman season was spent as a backup to Melvin Gordon and James White, who Clement would later play against in the Super Bowl. Even as the third back, Clement saw some action and finished his season with 547 yards and seven touchdowns while averaging 8.2 yards per game. His average yards per carry was good for the best out of his running back group.

After James White went to the NFL, Clement spent his sophomore season backing up Melvin Gordon. Gordon would go on to become the Big Ten Offensive Player of the Year, a unanimous All-American and the Doak Walker award winner after rushing for over 2,500 yards and totaling 32 touchdowns. Clement helped make Wisconsin one of the top-ranked rushing teams in the nation by adding nearly 1,000 rushing yards and nine touchdowns. Clement added a Big Ten Offensive Player of the Week award in his home state of New Jersey against Rutgers as well.

Clement put together an impressive season that was overshadowed by Gordon, who had a historical season.

Finally, in 2015, the show was all Clement's. A groin injury plagued Clement's season and he eventually needed sports hernia surgery. Clement played in just four games in what should have been his first season as the lead back. His lone 100-yard outing that season came against Rutgers, this time in Wisconsin. It was also the first three-touchdown game of his college career.

Clement rose to the occasion as a senior in 2016, leading the Badgers in yards from scrimmage and total touchdowns. In all but one game, the Glassboro native ran for at least 70 yards. He ran for at least 100 yards in eight games. Clement was the workhorse for the 10-3 Badgers and rushed for 71 yards and a touchdown in Wisconsin's Cotton Bowl victory over Western Michigan. Clement's final season as a Badger saw him total 1,375 rushing yards with 15 touchdowns.

Clement came out of Wisconsin with a knock that he couldn't catch the football, posting only 29 receptions in his four-year college career. According to his high school coach, that wasn't Clement's fault.

> "He did catch the ball," said former Glassboro High School coach Herb Neilio. "We ended up throwing the ball to him. For some reason Wisconsin I don't think did him any favors. He came out of college with this knock on him that he wasn't a pass-catcher but he always had good hands."

Clement came into Eagles training camp with an outside shot to make the roster. The Eagles already had LeGarrette Blount, Darren Sproles, Wendell Smallwood and fellow rookie (and fourth-round draft pick) Donnel Pumphrey. Clement did his part and made the Eagles opening day roster.

After Pumphrey began the season on injured reserve and Sproles landed on IR, Clement found himself as the third-string running back. The undrafted rookie made the most of his carries and led the team's running backs with six total touchdowns. Clement was scoring at a rate of once every 14 touches, best in the running back group.

Clement established his role as a red zone threat with all of his touchdowns coming from inside the 15 yard line. He averaged 4.3 yards per carry and 8.7 yards per reception inside the opponent's 20-yard line, huge chunks where the field is toughest to navigate.

Clement's best game came on the biggest stage, though. The running back, who had a knock on him for not being able to catch the ball out of the backfield, caught four passes to lead the team with 100 receiving yards and got into the endzone with a beautiful toe-tap touchdown in the back of the endzone. Not to mention that he was on the receiving end of the direct snap that began the "Philly Special."

Going from training camp body to active roster to Super Bowl hero is the most unlikely of stories for an undrafted rookie. Clement overcame the odds and made the wish of his 17-year-old self come true.

Nelson Agholor
Wide Receiver

13

Agholor spent the first five years of his life in Nigeria where his father was a professional soccer player. When he turned five, his parents and he moved to America and settled in Tampa, Florida where Agholor's uncle lived. It was in Tampa that Agholor's football life began.

The game of football helped Agholor overcome the culture barrier he faced as a child in a new country. The children in the neighborhood would play football in the street and this is where Agholor first learned about the game he would soon make his life.

As soon as he stepped foot on the field, Agholor was a star. At Berkley Prep high school he excelled at running back, nearly reaching 3,500 yards and 50 touchdowns in his junior and senior seasons combined. The high school running back's success led him to being graded as a five-star recruit. From the East coast to the West, Agholor committed to USC in the winter of 2012, 14 years after coming to America.

Just like with high school, Agholor's success was nearly immediate at USC despite being moved to wide receiver. He started as a backup but saw the field in all 13 of the team's games, totaling 340 yards on 19 receptions. In Agholor's freshman season, against the coach who would eventually draft him into the NFL, he had his third-highest receiving total of his college career. Against Chip Kelly's Oregon Ducks, Agholor made the most of a high-scoring affair and caught six passes for 162 yards – nearly half of his total for his entire freshman season.

In his first season as a starter, Agholor burst onto the scene. Agholor was named a second-team All-American for his punt return abilities. He averaged a USC-record 19.1 yards per punt return while taking two for touchdowns. He added a team-high 918 receiving yards on offense, finding the end zone six times.

It was in Agholor's junior season that he made his mark. After failing to top 100 receiving yards in the first six games, Agholor went on a four-game stretch of epic proportions. In a 3-1 stretch in October and November, Agholor had 40 catches for 674 yards and six touchdowns. Agholor's first round draft status could likely be attributed to those four games in which he put up a season's worth of stats.

Agholor's final stat line as a junior was one of the best in the country: 104 receptions, 1,313 yards, 12 touchdowns. Agholor was named first-team All-Pac12 after leading the conference in touchdown receptions and second and third in the conference in receiving yards and receptions, respectively.

The wide receiver's stock was so hot that he decided to forego his senior season and enter the NFL Draft. When the draft rolled around, Agholor became the fourth wide receiver taken with the 20th overall selection in the first round.

To this point, Agholor was anything but an underdog. As soon as he stepped on the field, football came natural to him and he dominated on offense for one of the biggest programs in college football. It wasn't until he reached the NFL did he have to overcome stacked odds.

Agholor joined a receiving corps in Philadelphia that had Jordan Matthews and Riley Cooper as starters with Josh Huff manning the slot position. With nearly identical measurables, Agholor was penciled in as the replacement for long-time Eagle Jeremy Maclin. Maclin had been the Eagles leading receiver in four of the five years prior to his free agency departure to Kansas City.

Agholor's arrival was anything but leading-receiver material. In his rookie season, a problem with drops appeared frequently. Officially, Agholor was credited with four drops on 44 targets in 2015. He finished the season with just 23 catches and 283 yards. The rookie got into the endzone just once. Despite being the fourth receiver taken in the draft he was 18th among rookie in receptions, 15th in yards and 18th in touchdown receptions.

Agholor proved in his rookie season that he was not yet ready to take the reigns as a lead receiver. Despite his lack of production in his rookie season, his snap percentage jumped from 58 percent in his rookie season to nearly 78 percent in 2016, the most among Eagles receivers. His target rate reflected this, reaching 69 targets. However, the drops were still an epidemic. He had 7 drops on the season – over 10 percent of his targets ended with one.

Agholor's struggles came to a head in following a week 11 matchup against the Seattle Seahawks. Agholor had a wide open drop and an illegal formation penalty that nullified a 57-yard Zach Ertz touchdown on back-to-back plays. The second-year receiver finished the game without a catch.

> *"I did it to myself," Agholor told the media in the locker room following the game. "I started getting into my own head and trying so hard and thinking about being perfect and when miscues were there and they were exposed, I let it just eat at me."*

It's an interview that is difficult to watch. Agholor was tormented by his mistakes. Doug Pederson benched Agholor the next week and he finished the season with just nine catches in the last seven games.

In two seasons, Agholor only caught 59 passes for 648 yards and three touchdowns. As the 20th overall pick, Agholor had fallen drastically short on the expectations put on him. With the drops plaguing the receiver, many had written him off.

Agholor entered his third NFL season with lowered expectations. Agholor was expected to be the team's third or fourth option behind Zach Ertz, Alshon Jeffery, and Torrey Smith. Without the pressure of being "the guy," paired with a move to the slot, Agholor flourished.

In 2017, Agholor totaled more receptions, receiving yards and touchdowns than his first two seasons combined. Additionally, the drops that plagued him were in the rearview mirror.

From the first offensive drive of 2017, which ended with a 58-yard Carson Wentz-to-Nelson Agholor touchdown, Agholor's confidence was at an all-time high. Agholor finished the season with 62 receptions for 768 yards and eight touchdowns.

Agholor's best performance of his career came against the Seahawks, almost a year after the game that caused him to be benched. In an Eagles' loss, Agholor shined with seven receptions for 141 yards and a touchdown. Both his receptions and yards were career-highs. The game, despite ending in a loss, was a personal redemption game for Agholor.

Agholor's career day kicked off a three-game streak in which he caught 22 passes for 264 yards and a pair of touchdowns. One of those catches came in a key moment against the Los Angeles Rams in which the Eagles clinched the NFC East. With Nick Foles in at quarterback and the Eagles facing a 3rd-and-8 with the lead and 1:46 to go in the game, the Eagles dialed up Agholor's number and he came up big. Just beyond the first down marker, Agholor laid out making an all-hands catch between two defenders and sealing the victory that clinched the division for Philadelphia. Not only is that a catch that 2015-2016 Agholor probably would have had deflect off his hands, it is a clutch situation that he likely never would have been called upon. Agholor's three-game stretch nearly totaled his rookie season numbers.

Agholor's production continued into the postseason when he had three receptions against the Atlanta Falcons ad added three more against the Minnesota Vikings. Agholor had 83 yards in the NFC playoffs. Agholor kicked it into another gear on the biggest stage. The third-year wide receiver led the team with nine receptions in the Super Bowl while accumulating 84 yards in a game that every yard mattered.

Three of Agholor's eight receptions came on the most important drive of the game. Trailing 32-33 late in the fourth quarter, the Eagles called Agholor's number on three consecutive plays. Agholor answered each call helping advance the ball from the Eagles' 48 yard line to the Patriots' 14 yard line with receptions of 10, 18 and 10 yards. The drive culminated with a Zach Ertz 11-yard touchdown catch and gave the Eagles a lead that they wouldn't surrender.

Against all odds and millions of fans, Agholor flipped the script and became an entirely different player in his third season than he was in his first two. He went from being a first-round pick to public enemy number one to one of the greatest redemption seasons in recent memory. The confidence displayed by Agholor in his third season in the league will only be bolstered by the new jewelry that accompanies a Super Bowl victory.

Alshon Jeffery
Wide Receiver

17

Alshon Jeffery's underdog story wasn't written until after the season had ended. Seventeen days after Jeffery made an acrobatic touchdown catch in the back of the endzone and the Eagles hoisted the Lombardi Trophy, Jeffery hit the surgery table. The Eagles prized free agent signing suffered a torn rotator cuff in training camp.

Jeffery was so sure of the Eagles potential, though, that he didn't let the injury sideline him. At the toughest position besides quarterback to play with such an injury, Jeffery fought his way through a 19-game season to help the Eagles reach the ultimate goal.

After turning down a multi-year offer from the Minnesota Vikings, Jeffery opted to sign a one-year deal with the Eagles. The opportunity to play with Carson Wentz drew Jeffery to Philadelphia. In a text exchange shortly after signing with the Eagles, Jeffery told Wentz that he was in Philadelphia to help Wentz win an MVP. Wentz responded that he didn't care about MVP and that all he wanted was a Championship. At that moment, Jeffery knew that the Eagles were onto something special.

Prior to joining the Eagles, Jeffery faced two tough seasons to close out his time with the Chicago Bears. In 2015, Jeffery battled various injuries and eventually ended up finishing the season on injured reserve. Despite the battles and only playing in nine games, Jeffery still led the Bears in receptions and receiving yards for the season.

Jeffery played the 2016 season under the franchise tag for the Bears. With three different starting quarterbacks and a 3-13 season, Jeffery closed out the season second on the Bears in both receptions and receiving yards.

To add to the poor season, Jeffery was suspended for games 10-13 for violating the NFL's performance enhancing drug policy. At the time of the suspension, Jeffery had just one 100-yard receiving game and one touchdown as the team's franchise player. When the Bears hit the reset button following the 2016 season, Jeffery was one of the players who didn't receive an offer to return to the Windy City.

Jeffery's fresh start came in Philadelphia where he would head into the season as the team's number one receiver. Jeffery's season got off to a slow start with his new team, topping 50 yards just thrice in the first seven games and catching just two touchdowns in that span. Many began to question if the Eagles got a bust with their big free agent signing of the season.

After hitting his stride and getting on the same page with his quarterback, Jeffery went on a six-game tear. In the Eagles next six games, Jeffery averaged 63 yards and a touchdown catch per game. In the process of that streak, Jeffery earned a four-year, $52 million extension from the Eagles, tying him to the team through the 2021 season.

After his slow start, Jeffery finished the regular season tied for third in the NFL with nine touchdown receptions and with the security of playing in one city for the foreseeable future.

Jeffery's hot streak continued into the playoffs where he averaged four catches for 73 yards and a touchdown in three games. Two of those scores came in the NFC Championship Game against the team who offered him more money and a longer deal than the Eagles prior to the season – the Minnesota Vikings.

Jeffery's last score of the 2017 season makes you wonder how someone with a torn shoulder muscle could have moved like he did. In the back of the endzone with a defender draped on his left side, Jeffery pulled in the touchdown reaching back and to his right. The 34-yard catch was the first touchdown of the game and set the tone that the Eagles would keep until the clock hit 0:00.

Jeffery's final stat line in 19 games may seem underwhelming for a team's number one receiver – 69 receptions, 1,008 yards and 12 touchdowns. However, when you consider the amount the Eagles spread the ball around (three players had over 50 catches, three players had more than 70 carries) and the typical recovery time for a torn rotator cuff (Eric Decker missed 13 games with the same injury in 2016), Jeffery's 2017 season was off the charts.

Like many of his teammates, Jeffery kicked it into another gear when it came to the biggest stage. His 34-yard touchdown was the Eagles second-longest pass play of the day and was the first touchdown of the evening.

In a season that started as underwhelming for the wide receiver, Jeffery's performance down the stretch paired with the news that he fought through a grueling injury for the entirety of the season proved that he fought like an underdog just like the rest of his teammates.

Brent Celek
Tight End

87

At the time of his release in March following the 2017 season, Celek was the longest-tenured Philadelphia athlete. He had flourished through the Andy Reid era, survived the Chip Kelly destruction and closed out his NFL career with Doug Pederson and a World Championship.

As a fifth-round pick in 2007, Celek came in as an unknown out of Cincinnati. In four years as a Bearcat, Celek only caught 91 passes for 1,135 yards. In a statistical outlier season in his sophomore year, Celek caught eight touchdown passes on 22 total receptions. While Celek saw improvements in both receptions and yards in his next two seasons, he maxed out at just 481 receiving yards as a senior. He only caught six more touchdown passes after his sophomore season. That season is tied for the most touchdown receptions Celek would have in any season in his career. As he entered the NFL there was an uncertainty to his what his role could and would be.

In his first two seasons, Celek served as a backup to veteran tight end LJ Smith. With Smith's departure following the 2008 season, Celek took over as the starter and had a breakout season in 2009.

In his third season, Celek quickly established himself as one of the best tight ends in the league. Among tight ends, Celek finished fourth in receiving yards (behind three Hall of Famers) and touchdown receptions. Number 87 was Donovan McNabb's top target that season with 14 more receptions than any other Eagle.

Celek's life at the top of the NFL tight end chain didn't last long, though. With McNabb's departure from Philadelphia, Celek quickly fell back down to earth the following season. He finished his season with just 42 receptions, 34 fewer than a year before. In his eight seasons following the breakout year, Celek topped 60 receptions just once more. The arrival of Chip Kelly in 2013 marked a new role for Celek.

The high-flying Eagles offense of 2013 saw Celek's highest yards per catch average (15.7) and the second-most touchdown receptions (6) of his career. Despite the uptick, Celek would eventually lose his starting position to Zach Ertz and would be relegated to the Eagles blocking tight end. From 2013 to 2017, Celek never caught more than 32 passes. He also saw his role cut in half, playing 76.5 percent of the offensive snaps in 2012 to a measly 38.7 percent in 2016.

While Celek's role as a target diminished, his importance was paramount as the Eagles had a rash of injuries to the offensive line almost every season. As the team's "sixth offensive lineman," Celek endeared himself even more to the "lunch-pailing" mentality of the city he played in.

As we've seen with some of his teammates earlier in this book and even more later, Celek stepped up big when it mattered most. After having just one reception throughout the playoffs, Celek threw the key block to create the running lane on LeGarrette Blount's 21-yard touchdown in the Super Bowl. The touchdown gave the Eagles a 15-3 lead.

One month and five days after the Eagles paraded down Broad Street, with Celek dawning a vintage Harold Carmichael jersey, the tight end was released by the Eagles to avoid a $5 million cap hit. It wasn't just a routine release by the Eagles. The organization issued a statement to go along with the roster move.

The statement tells you all you need to know about the tight end:

> "Brent Celek defines what it means to be a Philadelphia Eagle. His dedication to his profession and this organization is unmatched and he will go down as one of the best tight ends in franchise history. Brent embodied the City of Philadelphia's temperament and character with his toughness and grit. He has been a huge part of everything we have been building over the last decade, and it is only fitting that he was able to help us win our first Super Bowl last season.

> "Unfortunately, in this business we are forced to make difficult decisions, especially this time of the year. This one is as tough as they come, but in our eyes, Brent will always be an Eagle."

In Celek's eleven seasons in Philadelphia he missed just one game.

Celek announced his retirement from the NFL on August 31st, 2018, having been a member of the Eagles for the entirety of his career. The tight end will be forever an Eagle, especially after helping to bring a ring to the City of Brotherly Love.

Trey Burton
Tight End

Trey Burton has faced plenty of ups and downs throughout his football career and has experienced the ultimate up of winning a World Championship at the highest level of football. However, he had to fight through those downs to get there.

Burton was a superstar at Venice High School and got recruited by the University of Florida and Urban Meyer. After an incredible freshman season, Meyer left and Burton was stuck in limbo without a true position. His three seasons without direction made him undraftable in the eyes of the NFL. When he did get his shot in the NFL he only touched the ball eight times in his first two seasons. Then, Doug Pederson came along.

Burton's football career began in Florida where he was a dual-threat quarterback at Venice High School. In his junior and senior seasons he rushed for a combined 46 touchdowns while throwing for 30 touchdowns. Even as the football powerhouse state that Florida is, Burton was an all-state selection both seasons.

Burton was recruited to the University of Florida as a spread offense quarterback. However, during his time in college he threw just 17 passes. Burton played running back, tight end, wide receiver and a quarterback while a Gator. His role on offense began as a running back and focused less on running and more on receiving as the years progressed.

As a freshman, it looked like the Gators may have recruited a Heisman candidate. Just four games into his collegiate career, Burton broke Gators' legend Tim Tebow's school record for touchdowns in a game with six. Against Kentucky, he ran the ball five times for five touchdowns. He also caught a touchdown pass in the first quarter of the 48-14 blowout victory. As if six touchdowns weren't enough, Burton also completed his only pass attempt for 42 yards.

After a 12-touchdown freshman year in 2010, Burton was unable to find a steady role when Will Muschamp took over as head coach in 2011. Burton saw his rushing attempts, receptions and touchdown production fall each of his next two seasons before finding a role as the team's third receiver in his senior season. He caught 38 passes for 445 yards but only got into the endzone once.

The change in coach from Meyer to Muschamp proved to be detrimental to Burton. Without a steady position or production, Burton went undrafted in the 2014 NFL Draft.

Chip Kelly and the Eagles gave Burton his shot in the NFL as an undrafted free agent when he signed a three-year deal.

In his first two seasons in the NFL, Burton was almost exclusively a special teams player, touching the ball on offense just eight times through 2015. It wasn't until Pederson came to Philadelphia that Burton saw extensive action on offense.

The former Gator caught 37 passes for 327 yards and a touchdown in his third season, his first with Pederson. In 2017, he had a nose for the endzone, scoring five times on only 23 receptions. At a clip of one touchdown per 4.6 touches, Burton was by far the most efficient Eagle in terms of making the most of his touches.

Burton was largely quiet in the playoffs, hauling in just one pass for 12 yards against the Vikings in the NFC Championship. When the Eagles called Burton's number in the big game, he delivered on a play that will go down in Eagles history.

The success of The Philly Special was reliant on a touch pass from a tight end who hadn't completed a pass since 2012. Burton's teammates implored him to not throw the pass too hard, Foles wasn't used to catching passes. His coaches told him options one, two and three were to run the ball after receiving the pitch from Corey Clement. Months after the conclusion of the Super Bowl victory, Head Coach Doug Pederson revealed that the first practice attempts of the play, Burton sailed the ball well over the quarterback's head. When Burton saw Foles without a defender in sight, he let it fly. The pass was perfect and resulted in one of the most memorable touchdowns in Super Bowl history.

Burton hardly saw the field in his first two years with the Eagles. When Pederson came to town, Philadelphia saw what the tight end had to offer. When his number was called in the Super Bowl, the world saw what the tight end had to offer.

Lane Johnson
Right Tackle

65

For a player who didn't know his true position until he was 21 years old, Lane Johnson has become an elite right tackle in the NFL after being selected fourth overall in 2013.

Johnson was an All-District quarterback in his home state of Texas and was an honorable mention All-State selection. He went on to play a year of junior college football at Kilgore College where he played quarterback and tight end. Johnson transferred to Oklahoma and red-shirted the 2009 season. He then played tight end and defensive end as a sophomore. Finally, as a junior, Johnson found his home on the offensive line. By his senior season, his second as an offensive lineman, he was named All-Conference and a third-team All-American by one media outlet.

During pre-draft workouts Johnson solidified his position as a top-ten pick. The former quarterback, tight end and defensive lineman was selected behind Eric Fisher, who has played well for the Chiefs, and Luke Joeckel, who couldn't quite cut it as a tackle in the NFL and has made the move to guard for the first time in his football career. Johnson, the 2017 first-team All-Pro, has far out-played the two offensive linemen selected ahead of him.

Johnson has not been without faults, himself, though. In his sophomore season in the NFL he tested positive for performance-enhancing drugs and was suspended the first four games of 2014. The Eagles started 3-1 but there was a target now on the back of Johnson. Another slip-up could mean huge penalties.

After a stellar 2015 campaign, Johnson's second slip up cost him ten games of the 2016 season. Another positive PED test came just seven months after Johnson signed a six-year contract extension that averaged $10.5 million per year.

Not only was the suspension detrimental to Johnson, it also effected rookie quarterback Carson Wentz and his development. Johnson fought the suspension to no avail and served his suspension from week six to week fifteen. The team was 5-1 when Johnson played and just 2-8 during his suspension.

While Johnson's absence showed how important he was to the team's success, it also meant he was one mistake away from potentially derailing his career. The right tackle was apologetic but was in the doghouse, so to speak, of many Philly faithful.

When Johnson returned in 2017, he told the media that he had a lot to make up to Eagles fans. He said in July, should the Eagles win the Super Bowl over the next few years, he would buy beer for everyone. Little did he know then that his promise would come to fruition just six months later. Luckily for Johnson, the promise didn't hit his pockets as Bud Light promised to pick up the tab should the Eagles win the big game.

Johnson went on to be named First-Team All-Pro and be named to his first Pro Bowl. He was one of the best offensive linemen in the league, definitely making his previous wrongdoings up to any fans who still held it against him.

Along with Chris Long, Johnson was instrumental in bringing the underdog moniker to the Eagles. The duo bought dog masks prior to the divisional playoff game against the Falcons, had Jason Peters hold them in his jacket for the game, and dawned them as they walked off the field in victory. The masks and the team heading to the Conference Championship led to Amazon selling out of and restocking the masks multiple times over the next week from thousands of fan purchases.

After being the fourth overall pick in 2013, Johnson has faced some lows with a pair of positive PED tests and a total of 14 games lost to suspension. He promised to make it up to fans and did more than his part in helping bring the Lombardi Trophy to Philadelphia.

Jason Kelce
Center

62

Kelce has had quite a ride with the Philadelphia Eagles. Coming in as a sixth-round pick in 2011, Kelce battled Jamaal Jackson, who was injured in 2010 but was the full-time starter the four years prior, and won the starting center position heading into his rookie season. He started all 16 games for the Eagles in his rookie year.

Kelce's path to being an elite NFL center was a unique one. As a running back and linebacker, Kelce was named an All-Lake Erie League selection twice in high school. Without any scholarship offers at the conclusion of his high school career, Kelce successfully walked on at the University of Cincinnati as a linebacker.

At 6-3 and 240 pounds coming out of Cleveland Heights High School, with experience in the backfield, the switch was quickly made for Kelce to play fullback. After redshirting his freshman year, Kelce finally made the switch to where he would make his career; the offensive line.

Kelce saw action in nine games in 2007 and started all 13 games in 2008 as the team's left guard. Kelce helped pave the way for a Bearcats offense that averaged nearly 400 yards per game and won the Big East. Cincinnati went on to lose the Orange Bowl to Virginia Tech 20-7.

In 2009, Kelce and the Bearcats continued their dominance and went undefeated in the regular season before losing the Sugar Bowl to Florida. Kelce was named to the first of two second-team All-Big East rosters.

It wasn't until 2010 that Kelce saw his first action at center and while he fit right in, earning All-Big East honors and an honorable mention All-American, the Bearcats didn't sustain their success from years past. With a new coach at the helm, Cincinnati went 4-8 and Kelce's college career concluded on a low note and with just 12 games at the position he hoped to play at the next level.

Despite running the fastest 40-yard dash among offensive linemen at the NFL Combine, Kelce's 6-3, 280-pound physique lacked "NFL size," according to a lot of analysts. Kelce was overlooked for 190 picks, falling to the Eagles in the sixth round. Being selected by the Eagles could have been the best thing to happen to Kelce in his career, though.

With Howard Mudd newly in position as the offensive line coach, Kelce would study under the coach who helped make another undersized center, Jeff Saturday of the Indianapolis Colts, into a six-time Pro Bowler and two-time First Team All-Pro. Mudd's specialty was with smaller, quicker offensive linemen, something the Eagles were transitioning to when he became the offensive line coach in 2011.

> *"I have been surprised by how much I have learned so far," Kelce told Lehigh Valley Live during training camp in 2011. "Jamaal [Jackson] has done a lot to help me. I think I fall into the mold of what [Mudd] likes: short, quick and athletic linemen."*

After winning the starting center position, Kelce became the first rookie in Eagles history to start all 16 games at center. The Eagles finished just 8-8 but Kelce and the offensive line helped running back LeSean McCoy lead the league and break the franchise record for touchdowns in a season with 20 total scores.

In 2012, Kelce tore his ACL and MCL in the second game of the season and missed the remainder of the year.

When he returned in 2013, he came back to a new head coach and offensive line scheme. He was a perfect fit for Chip Kelly's fast-paced, high-speed offense. He helped pave the way for another historic season for LeSean McCoy, who had over 1,600 yards. Kelce finished the year as Pro Football Focus's top-rated center.

Following the 2013 season the Eagles rewarded Kelce with a six year contract extension worth $37.5 million. Despite being instrumental in two historic rushing seasons for McCoy, Kelce had yet to be named to a Pro Bowl. That changed in 2014 with new contract in hand and despite missing four games after sports hernia surgery. Eagles' running backs combined for 1,820 rushing yards and 15 touchdowns in 2014. The Eagles offense finished in the top ten in rushing for the second year in a row and the third time in the four years Kelce had been with the team.

Despite continuing to play at a high level and one of the few consistencies in the Eagles offensive line, Kelce seemed to be Philadelphia's least wanted over the next few seasons. Kelce was the subject of countless trade rumors through 2015 and 2016. Those rumors became loudest before the 2017 season despite Kelce being named to his second Pro Bowl in 2016. Kelce seemed to use that as motivation, coming in and being dominant once again, earning his first All-Pro honors.

Of course, Kelce's 2017 season will forever be remembered for his passionate speech on the Art Museum steps following the Eagles Super Bowl Parade. Kelce had some choice words for national media "experts" who counted the Eagles and their players out, naming 24 of his teammates, including himself, and what media members negatively said about them.

> "Howie Roseman, a few years ago, was relinquished of all control pretty much in this organization. He was put in the side of the building where I didn't see him for over a year. Two years ago, when they made a decision, he came out of there a different man. He came out of there with a purpose and a drive to make this possible. And I saw a different Howie Roseman. An underdog.

> "Doug Pederson. When Doug Pederson was hired, he was rated as the worst coaching hire by a lot of freakin' analysts out there in the media. This past off-season, some clown named Mike Lombardi told him he was the least-qualified head coach in the NFL. You saw a driven Doug Pederson, a man who went for it on fourth down, went for it on fourth down, in the Super Bowl, with a trick play. He wasn't playing just to go mediocre. He's playing for a Super Bowl.

> "And it don't stop with him. It does not stop with him.

> "Jason Peters was told he was too old, didn't have it anymore. Before he got hurt, he was the best freaking tackle in the NFL. Big V [Halapoulivaati Vaitai] was told he didn't have it. Stefen Wisniewski ain't good enough. Jason Kelce is too small. Lane Johnson can't lay off the juice. Brandon Brooks has anxiety.

> "Carson Wentz didn't go to a Division I school. Nick Foles don't got it.

"Corey Clement's too slow. LeGarrette Blount ain't got it anymore. Jay Ajayi can't stay healthy.

"Torrey Smith can't catch. Nelson Agholor can't catch.

"Zach Ertz can't block. Brent Celek's too old.

"Brandon Graham was drafted too high. Vinny Curry ain't got it. Beau Allen can't fit the scheme.

"Mychal Kendricks can't fit the scheme. Nigel Bradham can't catch.

"Jalen Mills can't cover. Patrick Robinson can't cover.

"It's the whole team. It's the whole team."

The speech was a culmination of the team's underdog mentality. Kelce could have been the first player to win Super Bowl MVP four days after the Super Bowl.

Kelce revealed a quote that was on the wall of the Eagles offensive line room: "Hungry dogs run faster." The quote had been on the wall since 2013 and proved to be trust during the 2017 Super Bowl run.

Despite countless trade rumors and making it through three head-coaching regimes, Kelce has cemented himself as a legendary Eagle not only for his play on the field but for his leadership in the locker room and in Mummer regalia during the Super Bowl parade.

Jason Peters
Left Tackle

71

If you had to choose one current Philadelphia Eagle who will be enshrined in the Pro Football Hall of Fame at the conclusion of their career, Jason "The Bodyguard" Peters is the only choice. Peters' path to excellence is yet another underdog story.

After starring in basketball and football in his Texas high school, Peters attended the University of Arkansas, the only school who made the high school defensive end an offer. Recruited as a defensive tackle, Peters played in ten games and caught two passes while lining up at tight end in the 2001 season. After officially making the switch to tight end, Peters caught four passes in his sophomore season while playing in all 13 games.

Through 23 college games, Peters caught just six passes and failed to get into the endzone. It wasn't until his junior season that he started to show some flashes. He finished the season third on the Razorbacks in receptions, with 21, and receiving touchdowns, with four. Peters' stat line was enough to earn him second-team All-SEC honors. It wasn't enough, however, to solidify his position in the NFL.

At 6'4.5 and 328 pounds, Peters spent the majority of the 2004 NFL Combine Peters working out as an offensive lineman. Despite performing well during workouts, the lack of collegiate work on the offensive line concerned NFL scouts enough to not draft Peters. Following the NFL Draft, Peters signed with the Buffalo Bills as an undrafted rookie free agent tight end.

Peters failed to make the final cuts for the Bills but signed to the practice squad where he stayed until November. The Bills still didn't have a position for him but special teams coach Bobby April was happy to use the massive man who ran a sub-5.0 40-yard dash on his unit. The move paid dividends on December 19th when Peters blocked a punt and recovered it for a touchdown in a 33-17 victory over the Cincinnati Bengals.

While working heavily on special teams, Bills offensive line coach Jim McNally got his hands on Peters early, knowing that as athletic as he was, he was a project worth developing into a tackle. McNally coached through six decades and spent 27 years as an NFL offensive line coach.

In 2005, Peters got his shot at right tackle in a game against the defending Super Bowl Champion New England Patriots. Once Peters got his shot, he never looked back. Since 2005 Peters has started every game he has played in; 165 games. The first 16 of those starts came at right tackle. The rest came at left tackle, the most important position on the offensive line.

After two Pro Bowl seasons on the left side, the Eagles made a blockbuster deal in 2009 that brought Peters to Philadelphia in exchange for first-, fourth- and sixth-round picks. After making the trade, the Eagles voided the final two years of Peters' Bills contract and signed him to a six-year, $60 million contract.

> "Jason Peters is the best left tackle in football," said head coach Andy Reid at the time of the signing. "He is a powerful and athletic tackle and I have admired his play over the last few years on film."

The trade could be lauded as one of the best roster moves in Eagles' history as Peters solidified his Hall of Fame status as a member of the Eagles.

Peters has been a Pro Bowler in each season with the exception of 2012, when he missed the entire season, and 2017 when he missed nine games. He has blocked for twelve Philadelphia Eagles quarterbacks in his nine seasons with the team. He has been the heart and soul of the Eagles since joining the team and has been an unwavering presence both on the field and in the locker room.

A moment that will stand out in Peters' Eagles career came in 2014 against the Washington Redskins. Defensive tackle Chris Baker made a cheap-shot, blindsided hit to quarterback Nick Foles after a play had concluded. Peters was the first player to confront Baker, throwing a punch and getting ejected in the process. The reaction initiated a benches-clearing brawl on the sideline. The Eagles went on to win the game 37-34 despite losing Peters.

When Peters went down with an ACL-MCL injury against the Redskins in 2017, ending his season, the entire Eagles team surrounded the cart he was exiting on. Peters, as the cart pulled away, was coaching his replacement, Halapoulivaati Vaitai.

He is the true definition of the motto of "team before self." Peters is as close to a sure-thing Hall of Famer as you can get and it all began as an underdog who didn't have a position his first two seasons in the NFL. If there as one Eagle who deserved a ring, it was Peters.

Brandon Graham
Defensive End

55

Ever since Brandon Graham took the football field the sport came naturally to him. Starting competitive football at just seven years old, Graham excelled at linebacker, guard, kicker and punter. Graham's underdog story doesn't begin until high school.

Graham was widely graded as the best high school player in the state of Michigan by his senior season. Making his mark as a linebacker, Graham was elected captain of the East team of the US Army All-American Bowl. With four tackles and a blocked field goal, Graham helped the East win 27-16.

Graham was the first player from the state of Michigan to be chosen to play in the US Army All-American Bowl. Due to this, he was unaware that he was in violation of state rule by playing in an out-of-state all-star game. Graham was forced to sit out the winter and spring seasons of sports at his high school. Due to the off time, Graham gained 40 pounds, eventually forcing him out of the position where he had received so many accolades.

At 295 pounds, Graham's freshman season at Michigan was spent at defensive end while he attempted to shed the weight he put on while he was away from sports. Graham played in ten games but struggled to regain the form that earned him so much recognition to this point in his football career.

By his sophomore season, Graham was back down to 262 pounds and back in his old position on the defensive line. At just 19 years old, Graham started six games at defensive end. He helped the Wolverines spark an eight-game win streak by notching five combined sacks, seven tackles and two forced fumbles against rivals Notre Dame and Penn State in back-to-back weeks.

Graham continued his dominance at the collegiate level just as he did as a seven-year-old all the way through his high school career. Graham finished his career with eight games of at least three sacks including capping off his Michigan career with a four-sack game against Wisconsin and a five-sack game against Ohio State. Graham finished his four-year career with 29.5 sacks, 56 tackles for loss, a Big Ten MVP award and a first-team All-American selection in 2009. As if that weren't enough, Graham added a Senior Bowl MVP after tallying five tackles, two sacks and a forced fumble in the annual game.

Any NFL personnel member with a head on his shoulders knew that Graham was a top prospect and a no-doubt-about-it first round selection. The Eagles made that selection when they came on the clock at 13th overall in the 2010 NFL Draft.

Graham's first two seasons in the league were tough ones as he suffered a torn ACL toward the end of his rookie season after notching just six starts. He was unable to get back to football until November of the 2011 season. Graham started just seven more games from 2012 to 2014 which led many Eagles fans to label the first round pick a bust. In that same time period, Earl Thomas, a name many fans were calling when the Eagles were on the clock in the 2010 draft, was named a first-team All-Pro each season. Graham, meanwhile, was playing out of position and was already on his fourth defensive coordinator by the time the 2013 season came.

At the conclusion of Graham's rookie contract the Eagles elected to allow him to test free agency. Prior to the 2015 season, Graham visited with one team before signing a four-year extension with the Eagles. He later revealed that team to be the New York Giants.

With a new contract, Graham was motivated and quickly took to proving Eagles fans and "bust" labelers wrong. With 10 starts in 2015, the most of his career, Graham also had career-highs in sacks (6.5) and tackles (51). He solidified his position on the Eagles defense but was in for yet another change of coordinator and change of position.

Graham moved back to his original position on the defensive line as a defensive end when head coach Doug Pederson brought in Jim Schwartz to lead his defense. Graham fought for six seasons and listened to the criticism for years before having his breakout year in his seventh season as a 28-year-old defensive end.

The former Wolverine started all 16 games for the Eagles and again had a career-high in tackles with 59. A stout run-stopper, Graham accounted for 14 tackles for loss, the best on the team and the fourth-most in the NFL. Adding 6.5 sacks, Graham finally got national attention for the first time since his days at Michigan and was named second-team All-Pro.

Graham followed up his first All-Pro season with an even better one. Only this time, much like his team, he was overlooked and snubbed of a Pro Bowl berth or All-Pro selection. The defensive end opened the season with a pair of sacks against the Washington Redskins. He continued the tradition of one-upping himself by having a career- and team-high 9.5 sacks, 16 tackles for loss and scoring the first touchdown of his career in a game that clinched the NFC East for the Eagles.

Graham's role with the Eagles has evolved drastically over his eight seasons with the team. From trade bait to forgotten to bust to team leader, Graham's experience has led him to be a mentor for many of his teammates.

The shining moment of Graham's career to this point came in the waning moments of Super Bowl LII. Graham was the catalyst of arguably the biggest play in the franchise's history. Graham, lined up as a defensive tackle, bullied his way through Patriots' guard Shaq Mason to make his way to Tom Brady. With a five-point lead and under three minutes to play, the Eagles were in dangerous territory with Brady having possession of the ball. Graham changed that in an instant by getting to Brady and forcing the quarterback to fumble into the arms of Eagles' rookie Derek Barnett. The fumble was Brady's first in the playoffs since 2013.

It is no coincidence that the biggest play of the Eagles underdog season came from one of the biggest underdogs on the roster.

Malcolm Jenkins
Safety

27

Malcolm Jenkins was not good enough to play cornerback in the NFL. He wasn't good enough to be signed by the team that drafted him after his rookie contract expired. He was ranked the 37th-best free agent available and had six defensive backs who were more sought-after than himself in 2014. He wasn't good enough to get a contract like TJ Ward or Jairus Byrd, both of whom have been released by the teams that signed them in 2014. Jenkins has been an underdog since he entered the NFL.

As a New Jersey native, Jenkins played high school football at Piscataway Township High School. He helped his team to the state championship three years in a row as a wide receiver and defensive back. Despite the championships and the national attention, Jenkins was just a three-star recruit. His decision came down to staying in-state and going to Rutgers or attending Ohio State. Jenkins chose the latter and proved that his three-star rating was way off.

As a cornerback, Jenkins played mostly in the nickel as a freshman and tallied 37 tackles. When he was promoted to starter in his sophomore season he put the nation on notice. Jenkins had a nose for the ball, intercepting four passes and bringing the ball carrier down for a loss 4.5 times. His stellar play assisted the Buckeyes to an undefeated regular season and earned the first of three first-team All-Big Ten selections.

Jenkins' and Ohio State's dominance continued during his junior season as the Buckeyes went 11-1 in the regular season. Jenkins again had four interceptions adding 47 tackles and five tackles for loss. For his efforts he was named a second-team All-American in addition to his first-team All-Big Ten selection.

As a senior, Jenkins and the Buckeyes were 10-2 and suffered their third consecutive bowl game loss to close out the season. Jenkins' senior season was his best. He intercepted three passes and was a consensus All-American as well as the Jim Thorpe Award winner, given to the top defensive back in the nation.

Jenkins' college career undoubtedly showed that he was ready to take the NFL by storm. However, a subpar 40-yard dash had some question whether he would be a cornerback or a safety in the NFL. The New Orleans Saints selected Jenkins with the 14th overall pick as a cornerback.

Jenkins career at cornerback lasted just one season. His rookie season at cornerback saw his first career interception and four pass defenses while starting six games. Jenkins rode his way to the Super Bowl his rookie season and recorded five tackles in the victory over the Indianapolis Colts.

When the Saints drafted another cornerback in the first round in 2010, Jenkins was moved to safety. The move turned out to be the best thing for Jenkins' career. Over the next four seasons Jenkins recorded five interceptions while deflecting 34 passes.

In the final season of his rookie deal, Jenkins and the Saints met Chip Kelly and the Eagles in the Wild Card Round of the playoffs. Jenkins recorded three tackles in what would be his interview for his next job.

During 2014 free agency Eagles fans clamored for players like TJ Ward or Jairus Byrd, as mentioned above. Jenkins, however, wasn't on anyone's radar. The Eagles took a chance on Jenkins as a free agent and it paid off big time.

Jenkins was an instant starter in Philadelphia and his career saw a resurgence with his new team. For the first time in his career Jenkins started all 16 games and saw career highs in interceptions and pass deflections.

Despite the turmoil that came in the 2015 season with front office shake-ups and a head coach firing, Jenkins had his best season as a pro. Jenkins finished the season with two interceptions, three forced fumbles and 104 tackles. One of those interceptions came against Tom Brady in a December victory in which Jenkins returned the interception 99 yards for a touchdown. Jenkins had emerged as a leader of the Eagles defense and earned a first-team All-Pro selection and a Pro Bowl.

Jenkins was rewarded following the impressive season when a new regime took over in Philadelphia. In one of the new regime's first moves, they resigned Jenkins to a four-year extension locking him to Philadelphia through the 2020 season. Jenkins paid back the favor by tying his career-high in interceptions and returning two for touchdowns.

The 2017 season was routine for Jenkins. He started all 16 games for the fourth season in a row and intercepted two passes and recorded 69 tackles. As the leader of one of the top defenses in the NFL, Jenkins earned his second Pro Bowl. Jenkins proved to be one of the most important cogs in the Eagles' defense and had become the vocal leader of the team. In his four seasons in Philadelphia, he hadn't missed a game.

Jenkins' shining moment of the season came in the Super Bowl. Early in the second quarter, Patriots' wide receiver Brandin

Cooks caught a deep pass on the left side of the field and as he attempted to make a defender miss, he neglected to check his rearview mirror, where Jenkins resided. Jenkins delivered his biggest hit of the season and completely blindsided Cooks, knocking him out for the remainder of the game.

Jenkins' post-game locker room speeches helped the Eagles overcome injuries and being underdogs for every post season game. The coiner of "We all we got, we all we need," Jenkins embodied the underdog mentality that helped the Eagles bring home their first Lombardi Trophy.

Jalen Mills
Cornerback

31

Jalen Mills is another Eagle who excelled as soon as he stepped foot on the football field. Although he was rated as just a three-star recruit out of high school, Mills received at least ten scholarship offers, electing to attend the newly-dubbed "DBack U," LSU.

Mills had big shoes to fill in 2012, joining the Tigers a year removed from Tyrann Mathieu and Morris Claiborne and two years removed from Patrick Peterson. Combined, that trio accounted for four first-team All-American selections, two Jim Thorpe Awards (top defensive back in the nation) and two Chuck Bednarik Awards (top defensive player in the nation).

Mills stepped right in as a true freshman and started all 13 games at cornerback for the Tigers. He accumulated 57 tackles with two interceptions. Mills' best season came as a sophomore when he intercepted three passes with 67 tackles. He also got plenty of action behind the line of scrimmage with three sacks and four tackles for loss.

With an abundance of talent at cornerback LSU elected to shift Mills to safety for his final two years of college. Mills performed admirably in his first season at the new position, intercepting one pass and tallying 62 tackles.

The lowlight of the year came when Mills was accused of second-degree battery, allegedly punching a woman. Mills denied the allegations but spent a night in prison in Baton Rouge before being released on bail, paid $1,000 of the victim's medical bills, entered a diversion program and was subject to psychiatric evaluation as well as drug tests. The charges were eventually dropped to a misdemeanor and Mills' girlfriend at the time later admitted it was her, not Mills, who assaulted the victim. The incident was not overlooked during the predraft process.

The hits continued for Mills in 2015 when he suffered a preseason injury causing him to miss the first six games of the season. A fractured fibula and torn ligaments in his ankle, both detrimental for a cornerback, dropped his draft status drastically. Following the 2014 season, Mills was rated as a top draft pick, likely not making it out of the first round. Mills elected to play his senior season, though, and despite overcoming the injury, his draft stock had already taken a hit.

Despite missing half of the season, Mills played so well down the stretch that he earned a first-team All-American selection, joining his predecessors with the honor.

Participating in the NFL Combine, Mills' 40-yard dash was a death sentence for cornerbacks. Just three cornerbacks ran worse times than Mills' 4.61. When the 2015 All-American fell to the seventh round, the Eagles took their shot and ended up striking gold. The Eagles selected one of the hardest-working players on the team when they drafted the cornerback.

Mills began 2016 as the team's fourth cornerback and earned two starts by the end of his rookie season. He won the hearts of Eagles fans during his first training camp when he showed up to practice with green hair and was dubbed the "Green Goblin," a moniker that has stuck with him since. The Green Goblin finished his rookie season with seven defended passes and a lot of promise for a seventh-rounder.

Coming into 2017, with the departure of both 2016 starting cornerbacks, Mills had his eyes set on one of the vacant starting cornerback positions. He had the early lead with his late-2016 performance still fresh in coaches' minds. After training camp Mills secured a starting position and got to work, showing flashes of elite cornerback ability.

Mills finished the season as one of the most targeted cornerbacks but held every receiver he faced in check. He also showed one of the most important traits in a young cornerback which is the ability to have a short memory. Mills could give up a touchdown but on the next drive if he deflected a pass he was quick to shrug his shoulders, wag his finger and let the receiver know who won that play.

One of Mills' best games came in the NFC Championship Game when the defense held a high-flying Minnesota Vikings offense scoreless after an opening drive touchdown. The Eagles defensive backfield held the duo of Stefon Diggs and Adam Thielen under 100 yards and neither found the endzone. Diggs and Thielen averaged a combined 140 receiving yards per game throughout the 2017 season.

Following the Eagles Super Bowl victory it was revealed that during the game Mills suffered a left hand injury that later required surgery. With a torn ligament in his hand, Mills refused to exit the game and finished the game with a soft cast. The toughness of the cornerback paid off as he led the team and the game with nine tackles. Mills has a unique souvenir from the victory with a surgery scar that he plans to incorporate into a Super Bowl LII tattoo.

The Eagles found a diamond in the rough and a steal in the seventh round of the 2016 draft. Mills finished his sophomore campaign with three interceptions, his first touchdown dating back to high school and fourteen defended passes. Mills started all 15 games he played in and the Eagles have a starting defensive back for the foreseeable future.

His swagger will endear him to Philadelphia Eagles fans as long as he is wearing midnight green.

Mychal Kendricks
Linebacker

95

Mychal Kendricks has had a nose for the football since he stepped foot on the gridiron. As a linebacker and running back at Hoover High School in Fresno, California, Kendricks was the star of the team. In his senior season he averaged 7.2 yards per carry and ran for 742 yards with six touchdowns. On the defensive side of the ball, Kendricks averaged almost 15 tackles per game that same season.

At the conclusion of his high school career, Kendricks had six offers of schools to attend. Recruited as a defensive lineman, Kendricks chose to become a Golden Bear and committed to Cal. As a freshman, Kendricks played in every game but was quiet on defense, only notching 15 tackles and one sack, a steep drop from his high school dominance.

A year later, Kendricks saw an uptick in his tackles and returned his first collegiate interception for a touchdown but still wasn't anything close to what he was in high school. It wasn't until his junior season that Kendricks received national attention and his numbers reflected it.

Kendricks was active behind the line of scrimmage in his junior season, tallying 15 tackles for loss to go with 8.5 sacks, the highest total of his career; high school, collegiate or professional. The linebacker added three fumble recoveries as well.

In 2011, Kendricks continued his dominance. With 14.5 tackles for loss, Kendricks totaled 106 tackles on the season with three sacks. He also added a pair of interceptions and two pass deflections, showing his versatility in the passing game. For his efforts, Kendricks was named the PAC-12 Defensive Player of the Year.

When draft day came, Kendricks didn't have to wait long to hear his name called. The Eagles selected him with the 46th overall pick in the 2012 NFL Draft and he was immediately named one of the starting outside linebackers.

Kendricks played the second-most snaps by a linebacker and the fourth-most on the team as a rookie. Starting 14 games, Kendricks deflected nine passes and racked up 75 tackles. In his second season, Kendricks flourished.

Kendricks was moved to inside linebacker with the installment of a 3-4 defense under new head coach Chip Kelly and defensive coordinator Billy Davis. At his new position, Kendricks finished the season second on the team with 113 tackles, behind only fellow inside linebacker DeMeco Ryans. Showing his versatility yet again, Kendricks intercepted three passes (the only three interceptions in his career to date), forced two fumbles, recovered four fumbles and added a career-high four sacks.

After a career year, Kendricks' role inexplicably diminished. Over the next two seasons Kendricks started 24 games and sacked the quarterback seven times and added 165 tackles. Despite the steady production, Kendricks snap count dropped from 82.6 percent in 2013 to 65.5 percent in 2014 and dropped again to 51.7 percent in 2015.

With another change in defensive scheme and a new head coach in 2016, Kendricks had his worst year as a pro. With defensive coordinator Jim Schwartz in position, Kendricks rarely saw the field as the Eagles played in nickel defense frequently. With Jordan Hicks and Nigel Bradham as the top two linebackers, Kendricks saw the field on just 26.7 percent of snaps and had a career-low 8 starts. The 26-year-old had just 28 tackles and failed to record a sack in the season for the first time since peewee football.

Kendricks' lack of play time and hitting a low point in his career forced him to request a trade. The Eagles were active in seeking a trade partner but ultimately retained Kendricks for the 2017 season.

All of that set up a comeback season in 2017 for Kendricks who played arguably the most consistent football of his NFL career. He proved to finish plays that he would let get by him in previous years. Notably, Kendricks secured many tackles against running backs one-on-one in the open field, a play that Kendricks has failed on so frequently in his earlier years. He looked like a new player in his limited role.

Kendricks' play-making ability showed up again in the pass game, recording his most pass deflections since his rookie year and making his presence felt as a pass rusher with two sacks, his first since early in the 2015 season. Due to Jordan Hicks' midseason injury, Kendricks' snap percentage increased to 59.5 percent, the highest since 2014. Kendricks proved to be reliable in the star's absence and played well alongside linebacker Nigel Bradham.

In the NFC Championship Game against the Minnesota Vikings, Kendricks led the team with eight tackles. Kendricks' parents were in attendance as his brother Eric was a starting linebacker for the Vikings. The older brother came out on top as the Eagles beat the Vikings 38-7 and punched their ticket to Super Bowl LII.

From stud young linebacker to forgotten on the bench to next man up, Kendricks fit right in with the theme of the Eagles' 2017 season.

Nigel Bradham
Linebacker

53

Nigel Bradham was dominant in his football career from his days in high school through his Florida State career. Bradham accumulated more than 400 tackles and 20 sacks at Wakulla High School in Florida, including two seasons of 145 tackles. Bradham was named a USA Today All-American and played in the 2008 US Army All-American Bowl. As one of the top recruits in the nation, Bradham had his choice of schools to attend.

Choosing to stay in his home state, Bradham elected to attend Florida State where he played from day one. Bradham played in all 13 games as a true freshman and brought down the ball carrier 29 times. His last three collegiate seasons were where Bradham continued his dominance. Bradham averaged 92 tackles and almost seven sacks per season including a career-high 9.5 sacks in his senior season, when he was a team captain. The linebacker led the Seminoles in tackles in each of his final three seasons.

Despite all of his success in his football career to this point, Bradham wasn't selected until the fourth round of the 2012 NFL Draft. Eleven linebackers were selected before him.

Bradham's high school and collegiate success didn't translate in his first two seasons with the Bills, starting just 13 games. After a rookie season that yielded 11 starts, Bradham was relegated to backup duties in his second season and earned just two starts.

After injuries and a shuffle on the defensive side of the ball, Bradham entered 2014 as the starting outside linebacker and started all 14 games in which he played. Bradham showed out with career-highs in almost every statistical category including 104 tackles and seven pass deflections. Bradham's career year was his first with Jim Schwartz as his defensive coordinator.

In 2015, without Schwartz, Bradham returned to below-average form as the Bills limped to an 8-8 season and Bradham missed the final five games of the season due to injury. Bradham entered free agency for the first time in his career following another subpar season in Buffalo.

When the Eagles hired Schwartz to be the defensive coordinator in 2016 he brought a number of his former players with him to Philadelphia. One of those players was Bradham, an under-the-radar signing who eventually played a huge role in the Eagles run to their first Super Bowl.

Bradham played three seasons under Schwartz between his 2014 season with the Buffalo Bills and his two seasons with the Eagles. There is a clear distinction between his seasons with and without the defensive coordinator leading the way. In three seasons without Schwartz, Bradham has averaged 52.3 tackles, 1.7 passes defensed, and 0.33 sacks per season. In three seasons with Schwartz, Bradham has averaged 97 tackles, 6.7 passes defensed and 1.8 sacks per season.

Despite an offseason incident in which Bradham assaulted a hotel worker, Bradham entered 2016 as the Eagles starting outside linebacker and, for the first time in his career, played in and started all 16 games. A season after finishing as Pro Football Focus's 79th-ranked linebacker, Bradham finished 2016 as the league's ninth-best linebacker. A below-average starter in Buffalo, Bradham quickly made his mark in Philadelphia and returned to the top of his game.

During the Eagles' bye-week in 2016, Bradham was caught with a loaded weapon at Miami International Airport. His second incident in seven months since becoming an Eagle sparked a response from his defensive coordinator.

> "If you do dumbass things, pretty soon you will be labeled a dumbass," said Schwartz. "He's got a lot of ground to make up. It's not just him. It's the rest of us. He represents everybody. He has to earn some trust back."

Bradham earned some of that trust back in 2017 when he continued the upswing of his career. Entering a week eight game against the division rival Washington Redskins, the Eagles were 6-1 and one of the best defenses in football. The victory to push them to 7-1 came at a price, though, as the Eagles lost the heart of their defense in Jordan Hicks. With Hicks out for the season with an Achilles injury, the responsibility on defense shifted to Bradham, who turned his game up a notch further.

With Hicks out Bradham took over as the defense's signal caller with the radio in his helmet with Schwartz on the other end. In addition, Bradham was relied on to be versatile, playing a variety of positions including his original weak side position as well as middle linebacker. In his expanded role the 28-year-old led the team in tackles with 88.

Bradham was a model of stability at a position that looked uncertain after Hicks' injury. Whether it were in the run game, dropping in coverage or getting the defense in position, Bradham was consistent across the board for the Eagles defense.

A below average starter in Buffalo, reuniting with Jim Schwartz and becoming a leader on defense pushed Bradham to a new level of play.

Bradham's first playoff experience came in 2017 and he made the most of it. In three games Bradham accumulated 15 tackles and a sack. His efforts included the team's third-most tackles in the Super Bowl with seven as the defense's playcaller.

Jake Elliott
Kicker

4

Full-ride scholarships are not easy to come by for high school athletes. Full-ride scholarships are almost non-existent when it comes to high school kickers. This was not the case for Jake Elliott, who was offered two scholarships out of high school and elected to attend the University of Memphis. It wasn't the last time Elliott would overcome the odds stacked against his position.

When Elliott arrived to Memphis he made it clear that he would be the kicker from the jump. The 18-year-old was 16-for-18 on field goals his freshman season including a school-record 56-yard bomb which broke a record set by future Super Bowl opponent Stephen Gostkowski in 2005.

Elliott came back down the earth in his sophomore season, converting just 21 of his 32 field goal attempts, a percentage of 65.6. For the second year in a row, Elliott was perfect on extra points, though, bringing his total to 81-for-81. In his final two years of college Elliott converted 81 percent of his field goals, bringing his collegiate career percentage to 77.9 percent.

At the conclusion of his career, Elliott held conference records for total points, extra points and field goals in conference history. He was also perfect on extra points, making 202-of-202.

Elliott's stellar college career earned him another honor not frequently bestowed upon kickers. In the fifth round of the 2017 NFL Draft, Elliott was drafted by the Cincinnati Bengals. The Bengals held an open competition for their starting kicker position which Elliott failed to secure. At the conclusion of the preseason Elliott was released and signed to the Bengals' practice squad.

When the Eagles lost kicker Caleb Sturgis to a season-ending injury in the 2017 season opener, they called upon Elliott. Nine days after Elliott landed on the Bengals practice squad, he was the starting kicker for the Eagles.

In his first NFL game, Elliott continued his perfect streak on extra points, hitting two-of-two but was just two-for-three on field goals. To say Elliott rebounded the following week would be an understatement.

On Elliott's first attempt of the day he missed a 52-yard field goal attempt. Following the miss, his second in as many games as an Eagle, NFL Films caught an exchange on the sideline between Jason Peters and Elliott.

> "Hey Elliott, come on, baby. No more misses, man. Let's go. No more misses. Hey, no more misses, bro."

The message got across to Elliott loud and clear. With 51 seconds remaining and the Eagles in need of a field goal to tie the game, Elliott was called on again. This time, from 46 yards out. The attempt was no chip shot in a high-pressure situation but Elliott nailed it. The Eagles forced a quick three-and-out by the Giants on the ensuing drive. A 19-yard reception by Alshon Jeffery on the Eagles final possession set up the chance for a hope and a prayer.

Once again, Elliott was called on to attempt a field goal. This time, it was for the game. This time, it was 61 yards. It had been three years and ten months since Elliott hit his 56-yard school record-breaker at Memphis.

With 0:01 on the clock, Elliott lined it up and snuck the 61-yarder just over the cross bar and just inside the right upright. The crowd erupted, the team stormed the field and Elliott was an instant superstar in the City of Brotherly Love. The kick was a franchise-record, rookie-record, game-winning-record blast. With his parents in attendance, Elliott was carried off the field by his teammates. In just his second NFL game, 12 days after becoming a member of an active NFL roster, Elliott was awarded Special Teams Player of the Week.

With Jason Peters' demands still in his mind, Elliott was a perfect 10-for-10 on his next ten kicks. Elliott missed just three kicks the remainder of the season and went on to hit 17-of-19 field goals of 40 yards or more during the regular season. He also made five field goals of 50 yards or more, the most in a season in Eagles history.

Elliott wasn't done after the regular season, either. The 23-year-old was a perfect seven-for-seven in the playoffs making the two longest field goals by a rookie in Super Bowl history. His 53-yard field goal to close out the first half against the Atlanta Falcons was the longest postseason field goal by a rookie in NFL history. Elliott rewrote the history books in his rookie season.

From draft pick to practice squad to playoff perfection, Elliott's rookie season began as an underdog and concluded with the highest of highs to go along with a long list of new records with his name on them.

Bryan Braman
Specialist

50

Bryan Braman? You're damn right Bryan Braman. The "kill, maim, destroy" special teamer spent the first thirteen weeks of the season sitting at home waiting for a call.

Braman has played the role of the underdog for the entirety of his NFL career, making a living on the third phase of the game: special teams. With Chip Kelly's affinity for special teams, Braman was brought to the Eagles in 2014. Upon his arrival, he described his style of play as "kill, maim, destroy," which immediately endeared him to Eagles fans. A quick YouTube search backed up Braman's claims when a 2011 highlight of Braman making a head-to-head hit without a helmet on shows up. Braman was a standout on special teams for the next three seasons, playing more snaps on special teams than any other Eagle. The Eagles let him walk following the 2016 season without making him an offer.

Braman was signed by the New Orleans Saints but was released two days before the start of the season with an injury. After being released, Braman went unsigned and was without a team for the first thirteen weeks of the season.

Braman stayed in football shape and was ready when the Eagles called to bring him back on December 12th. The Eagles used

Braman to fill the spot that was left void when quarterback Carson Wentz was placed on Injured Reserve.

The career special teamer made his presence felt in the playoffs. In a game that every play was crucial, Braman blocked a punt with less than a minute to go in the first half against the Atlanta Falcons in the Divisional Round of the playoffs. The block set the Eagles up at their own 28-yard line with 0:22 remaining in the first half. The Eagles, to that point, had only mustered six points. With the advantageous field position, the Eagles managed to get into field goal range after Torrey Smith caught a pass off of a defender's knee and Nick Foles hooked up with Alshon Jeffery with one second remaining on the clock.

Had the Eagles not kicked the field goal before the half the Falcons could have attempted a chip-shot field goal on the final play of the game and the Eagles Super Bowl run could have ended before it began.

Three weeks later, in Super Bowl LII, Braman made another crucial play at a crucial time. With under a minute to go in the game, the Patriots attempted a reverse on a kickoff return that Braman and the Eagles sniffed out immediately. Braman was the man in the face of Rex Burkhead who secured the tackle inside the ten yard line, making the Patriots' attempt at an improbable comeback even more difficult.

After what were probably the longest thirteen weeks of his life, Braman came back to his former team and played a critical role in a playoff run that ended with the team's first Lombardi Trophy.

****

About the Author

Brenden Peddigree has been a Philadelphia Eagles fan since he could comprehend what was happening on the gridiron. When he realized that he was never going to grow beyond 5'8" and a soaking-wet 150 pounds, he turned his attention toward writing about the game he fell in love with. Peddigree has written for publications from The Philadelphia Inquirer, GCobb.com, Philly Sports Network and more. He has interviewed countless players and coaches and has written comprehensive profiles on Vinny Curry and Merrill Reese, among others. When Brenden is not in the glow of his laptop at 2am on a weeknight he is likely extending the love of football to his two year old son. He can be found on Twitter at @BrendenP_NFL or can be reached via email at BPeddigree2011@gmail.com.

20,859 Days: An Underdog Story is the first published book by Brenden. He did not suffer the years without a championship as long as many other Eagles fans but the moment the clock finally hit 0:00 on February 4th, 2018 was one of the most memorable moments of his 25 years. Brenden felt the best way to commemorate the franchise's first Super Bowl-winning roster was by chronicling the underdogs who made up one of the biggest underdog teams in the city's history.

Made in the USA
Middletown, DE
04 September 2018